The Jesus Challenge

The Jesus Challenge:
21 Days of Loving God and Neighbor

The Jesus Challenge
978-1-5018-7934-0
978-1-5018-7935-7 eBook

The Jesus Challenge DVD
978-1-5018-7936-4

Also from Justin LaRosa
A Disciple's Path: A Guide for United Methodists (with James A. Harnish)
A Disciple's Heart: Growing in Love and Grace (with James A. Harnish)
Sent: Delivering the Gift of Hope at Christmas (with Jorge Acevedo,
Jacob Armstrong, Rachel Billups, and Lanecia Rouse)

the JESUS challenge

21 DAYS OF LOVING GOD AND NEIGHBOR

JUSTIN LAROSA

Abingdon Press
Nashville

THE JESUS CHALLENGE:
21 DAYS OF LOVING GOD AND NEIGHBOR

Library of Congress Cataloging-in-Publication data has been requested.

978-1-5018-7934-0

19 20 21 22 23 24 25 26 27 28 — 10 9 8 7 6 5 4 3 2 1
MANUFACTURED IN THE UNITED STATES OF AMERICA

To my wife, Caroline, who continually
teaches me about love.
Thank you for who you are.
I am grateful for the ways you love, encourage,
challenge, and believe in me.

CONTENTS

A "HOW-TO" NOTE FROM THE AUTHOR

Whether you are going through this study with a group or independently, I am thrilled for you to join me on this three-week journey. Over the next twenty-one days, we'll move from *forgetfulness to remembering*, from *distraction to intentionality*, and from *self-sufficiency to God-reliance* so that we are enabled to live our lives centered on loving God and loving others as ourselves.

The book includes an introduction and three chapters (one for each week), which are accompanied by daily devotionals. We will work our way through spiritual practices like centering prayer and *Lectio Divina*, and we will begin with an introduction to "Methodical Prayer." Practicing this form of prayer sets up a rhythm and method to our prayer life, something that I've found paramount to my relationship with God, and I encourage you to practice this every day of this challenge in addition to or as part of your devotional time. If a leader is studying with a group, he or she can find Leader Helps in the back, which will aid in cultivating discussion and offering structure to the group experience. At the conclusion of the twenty-one days, I pray that your journey with Jesus will be strengthened as you live out the Greatest Commandment and walk in the ways of love. Welcome to *The Jesus Challenge*!

INTRODUCTION

Following Jesus is hard.

If anyone tells you that it isn't, then they are misinformed or just plain lying. Christians believe that every single human is made in God's image—this is a gift from God that is bestowed, not earned. And because of that gift, every human has inherent worth and dignity. Along with trusting that humans are made in God's image, Christians believe that Jesus lived, died a brutal death on the cross, and then was resurrected from the dead for the forgiveness of sins as part of God's redemption plan. And here's the thing: believing it in our heads might be the easiest part of being a disciple. I mean, Scripture says that even demons believe it.* To be clear, I am not minimizing the importance of believing in Jesus Christ. Believing in the life, death, and resurrection of Jesus is the most profound and life-changing experience one could ever have. It matters now *and* later. But believing it in your head doesn't always equate with following him with your heart. Maybe that's what the book of James is asserting when it declares, "Faith without works is dead" (James 2:26 NASB).

Following Jesus Christ is challenging because belief requires some-thing of us. Teresa of Avila, the sixteenth-century mystic, is regarded

---

* See James 2:19; Luke 4:41.

as the source of these words: "Christ has no body now, but yours. No hands, no feet on earth, but yours. Yours are the eyes through which Christ looks compassion into the world. Yours are the feet with which Christ walks to do good. Yours are the hands with which Christ blesses the world."* We are invited to become Jesus in the world, but what does this really mean? Essentially, the world will know Jesus by the people who believe and follow him. You might be the only Bible that someone in your life ever reads. In other words, people like you and me should be imitating Jesus and striving to become more like him in this life as we prepare for the next. Theologians have called this process different things over the centuries. The Eastern Orthodox Church called it "theosis" or "divinization." The Wesleyan tradition calls it "sanctification" or "the way of salvation." But you certainly don't have to be a scholar, theologian, or even an intelligent person to follow Jesus. You don't have to have studied any deep-rooted theology or be able to list the many different atonement theories. In fact, those things sometimes can get in the way. You just have to follow. And that means saying yes to becoming a love practitioner for the rest of your life. Being a practitioner of love means we have to learn how to love God more intentionally, love our neighbors (and figure out who they are), and forgive our enemies. This book will equip you to take next steps on that journey.

The disciples dropped everything they knew when they said yes to follow Jesus.† Jesus' words and actions, the way he included and healed those on the margins, and his promises about a new kind of kingdom were compelling enough for men and women to leave their lives to be a part of something greater. The world hasn't been the same since. We can assume that the disciples didn't know all of what their yeses meant, but we can be sure that they were the first of many. Love is woven through Jesus' life, death, and resurrection. During their time following him, men and women grew in understanding about what it meant to believe in Jesus as the Son of God, and would discover what

---

* Order of Carmelites, "Teresa Avila Quotes," Order of Carmelites website, https://ocarm.org/en/content/ocarm/teresa-avila-quotes, accessed August 31, 2018.

† See Matthew 4:19-20; Mark 1:17-18; John 1:43.

following him in community actually looked like. Their journey had no shortage of twists and turns, joys and pains, storms and sunshine, or mountaintops and valleys. Nor will ours. The disciples frequently missed the point. We will miss the point too. They fell down and got back up, often to fall down again. We too will fall and rise many times as we follow Jesus. Their expectations about what kind of king Jesus would be, how his new kingdom would operate, and their roles within it drastically shifted over the three years as he marched toward the cross. Our expectations may drastically shift as the journey unfolds.

As Dietrich Bonhoeffer said in *The Cost of Discipleship*, "Costly grace is the gospel which must be *sought* again and again, the gift which must be *asked* for, the door at which a man must *knock*. Such grace is *costly* because it calls us to follow, and it is *grace* because it calls us to follow *Jesus Christ*. It is costly because it costs a man his life, and it is grace because it gives a man the only true life."[*]

Jesus made no promises that following him would be easy. In fact, he promised exactly the opposite. In three of the four Gospels, Jesus says that in order to follow him, disciples would have to deny themselves and take up their cross.[†] If that wasn't daunting enough, he says his followers must take a narrow road and enter a narrow gate, which only a few would find.[‡] How can we find it? By saying yes, believing in Jesus, and picking up our crosses as we travel the narrow road. How might we do that? Jesus says *love*.

Jesus was asked by a religious leader, "Teacher, which commandment in the law is the greatest?" He said to him, "'You shall love the Lord your God with all your heart, and with all your soul, and with all your mind.' This is the greatest and first commandment. And a second is like it: 'You shall love your neighbor as yourself.' On these two commandments hang all the law and the prophets" (Matthew 22:36-40).

---

[*] Dietrich Bonhoeffer, *The Cost of Discipleship* (New York: Touchstone, 1995), 45.

[†] See Matthew 16:24; Mark 8:34; Luke 9:23.

[‡] See Matthew 7:13-14 (NIV).

Jesus strongly states that these two capture all the teaching of the prophets and the fundamentals of the Law. This is our litmus test for how we are becoming like Jesus. Many Christians are familiar with this teaching. Churches have emphasized it over the last few decades, even using it as a mission statement and placing it on their marquees. The teaching is clear: you must love God and neighbor with everything you have. Seems simple, right? Profound truth often is. Yet, simplicity does not mean that becoming a love practitioner will be easy. Life will thrust us into situations that prompt important questions like, "Whom are we to love?," "How are we to love?," and "Who is my neighbor?" How we answer these questions in our heads and live them out will determine how faithfully we live out the Greatest Commandment.

But one thing is certain—staying in our heads is not an option as disciples. We don't have to have all of the beliefs and doctrines all worked out to begin. Our response to God's grace, which is God-enabled, supports a practical application. We respond to God's grace by loving with all of our heart, soul, and mind. We won't do it perfectly and, of course, it is easier said than done.

But while following Jesus is a daunting task, not for the faint of heart, cultivating deeper relationships by loving God and neighbor is possible. It is what disciples of Jesus Christ strive to do. To "center" our lives around love, intentionality is paramount. Effort, support, and encouragement are required. Christians have three supports that provide the scaffolding for this lifelong journey: the Holy Spirit, the church, and spiritual practices.

The Holy Spirit is our ever-present guide. The church should function as the hub of our faith, where we worship, are equipped, and are challenged and sent out to participate in the restoration of our families, communities, and world. Spiritual practices act as God's refining fire, not only keeping us connected to God and one another but also shaping us in the likeness of Jesus Christ. All three are essential in helping us be skilled love practitioners.

Love Obstacles

The scaffolding and faith enable disciples to counter the resistance and inertia that inevitably come as we live out our faith. But obstacles are an essential part of any worthy endeavor; and loving God and neighbor is the highest privilege and call there is. Sometimes the obstacles we encounter are easily perceived; other times they are subtle—but they are always formidable.

The three obstacles that I have experienced and witnessed during my years as a follower of Jesus and serving as clergy in a congregation are forgetfulness, distraction, and self-sufficiency. They come in all shapes, sizes, and forms. Everyone I know struggles with these blocks. They are like a gravitational force that pull us away from following Jesus Christ. All three in their own way begin to diminish people's commitment to engaging in spiritual practices, their participation in a faith community, and using their gifts to serve in the community. They water down our efforts to love God, neighbor, and enemy.

Obstacle 1: Forgetfulness

"Those who don't know history are destined to repeat it."

Early in my journey back to a relationship with God, I was listening to cassette tapes (yes, I am that old) by the Episcopalian priest John Claypool. I listened to almost all of his tapes. I mean hours and hours. His style, teaching, soothing voice, and life experience drew me in and piqued my curiosity to seek deeper relationship to know Jesus Christ. But from all those hours of listening, it was one sentence from a tape that has reverberated in my soul ever since. It was, "The essence of original sin is forgetfulness." I was blown away. I always struggled with feeling the stain of sin even after rededicating my life to Christ and reaffirming my baptism in the church. He was suggesting that it was forgetfulness rather than wickedness that was at the root of our separation. This blew me away. I have discovered that as we follow Jesus, we are prone to forget who God is, forget who we are, and forget who we are called to be. The Bible supports the claim of forgetfulness and history repeating itself. There is example after example of the people of God having amnesia. They forget God's goodness, his love, his call on their lives. God can do something mighty, powerful, and miraculous, but it won't be too long before memory loss sets in. It happened to the Israelites. The disciples and the churches in the New Testament forgot; and we are no different. Forgetfulness is a substantial block to intentionality of loving God, neighbor, and enemy.

For the next twenty-one days, we will remember and practice love.

Obstacle 2: Distraction

*"Distracted from distraction by distraction."**

T. S. Eliot wrote these words a long time ago. They still fit. Our culture is busier and more technologically connected than at any other time in history. The digital age promised fewer work hours, more efficiency, and a hyper-connected world. It has delivered on those promises—except for maybe fewer work hours. But not without cost. People are distracted and overscheduled. Disconnecting from technology is a constant struggle for everyone, and we don't yet know the long-term effects of gazing at electronics. But we have seen disconnected living—in both subtle and obvious ways—including in the spiritual life. Additionally, twenty-four-hour connectivity has delivered nonstop communication about conflict, polarization, and violence, perpetuating fear among many. While we will never go back to the days of rotary phones and answering machines, we must find ways to mitigate distracted living because distracted living diminishes our ability as Christ followers to live out Jesus' Greatest Commandment. Distraction is a gigantic hurdle.

For the next twenty-one days, we will practice love through focus.

Obstacle 3: Self-Sufficiency

"We regard God as an airman regards his parachute; it's there for emergencies but he hopes he'll never have to use it."†

---

* T. S. Eliot, "Burnt Norton," in *Four Quartets* (New York: Harcourt, 1943), 17.

† C. S. Lewis, *The Problem of Pain* (New York: Macmillan, 1947), 84.

Humans prefer self-sufficiency over God-reliance. Our instincts and culture cry out for rugged individualism and control over our lives. The more control we have, the better. Deep within us, there is a place that resists relying on anyone or anything, including God.

Life's turbulence shows us the folly in self-sufficiency and need for trust in God. Whether it be addiction, disease, the untimely death of a loved one, a fractured relationship, a job loss, a debilitating medical condition, or any other suffering we can't avoid, all can expose the lies that we are in control and we are the source of our giftedness. Then and only then will people come face to face with the reality of the power of God-reliance. Having relinquished the idea of self-sufficiency, the airman now has trust in the pilot and believes he will be guided to the destination safely.

When we give up the controls and recognize our own giftedness is a gift, it doesn't mean the flight will no longer be bumpy. All of our skills, strengths, and inner resources are still employed, but we are grounded in a belief, understanding, and experience that God is with us. As we pivot toward this surrender, it will lessen the obstacle to living the Greatest Commandment.

For the next twenty-one days, we will practice love by being God-reliant.

Antidotes to Obstacles

If forgetfulness, distraction, and self-sufficiency are what draw us away from love, Proverbs offers wisdom so that we can remain mindful, focused, and trusting:

> *My child, do not forget my teaching,*
> *but let your heart keep my commandments;*
> *for length of days and years of life*
> *and abundant welfare they will give you.*
>
> *Do not let loyalty and faithfulness forsake you;*
> *bind them around your neck,*
> *write them on the tablet of your heart.*

So you will find favor and good repute
in the sight of God and of people.

Trust in the LORD with all your heart,
and do not rely on your own insight.
In all your ways acknowledge him,
and he will make straight your paths.

—*Proverbs 3:1-6*

The obstacle of forgetfulness is amplified in verses 1 and 3. Keeping faithfulness and loyalty around our necks and written on our hearts helps us if we are distracted. And verse 5 suggests that as we trust God in the ways we go in life and not our own smarts, our way forward will be with God. In other words, as we increase our God-reliance and decrease self-sufficiency, we will more fully be able to live out the commandments of God.

Said in a different way, the antidotes to the big three are being **faithful** to spiritual practices; being **fruitful** in the ways and with whom we invest our time; and lastly, being **surrendered** to the results. Intentionality around these three will serve as anchors to the spiritual life, and will shape our thoughts and actions around Jesus during these next twenty-one days. This is the road map to loving God and neighbor with all of our heart, our mind, our soul, and strength.

If we want to love God with all of our heart, mind, soul, and strength, and diminish the gravitational pulls of forgetfulness, distraction, and self-sufficiency, then ordering our lives around spiritual practices, around the people who will go on the journey with us, and surrendering over and over again to the outcomes is a good road map for living. Again, simple, but not easy.

METHODICAL PRAYER

One way to meet the challenge of intentionally loving God with your heart, mind, soul, and strength is by creating a methodical discipline and rhythm to your prayer life. These tips will work in any season and can be tailored and adjusted. During the three weeks you spend with this challenge, you can add this as part of your devotional time, but the intention is that this will influence your prayer habit far beyond the 21 days spent with this book. I suggest setting aside fifteen minutes at a minimum. But no matter what, just do it.

In preparation, you will create a gratitude list and designate a time and place that is free from distractions. When possible (and if you are able), this place should allow you to pray on our knees and speak to God aloud in your own voice. During the time you set for this practice, you will read Scripture, pray for people in your life, name the things for which you are grateful, and confess your blocks (sins). Lastly, you will end with the Lord's Prayer.

Gratitude List

Get out a sheet of paper, a journal, or your phone. Spend time reflecting on your life. What are the circumstances that make your heart sing? Who are the people who love you? What about the things you have, your job, relationships, your children, pets, health? Include things large and small, ordinary and extravagant. Take as much time as you need, and make the list as comprehensive as possible. You'll refer to the list during your prayer time each day and be thankful to God for these things.

Place and Time

Decide in advance when and where you will spend time in prayer loving God. Remember, that's what you are doing! Feel free to pray all throughout the day, but set aside intentional time alone in a designated time and place. You may already have a spot and time that works. It could be in the morning at the dining room table, in the school parking lot while picking up the kids, or in the evening in a room by yourself. Wherever possible, select a time and location where distractions are minimal.

On Your Knees

If you are physically able, start your prayer time on your knees. Most churches have extinguished the practice of having the congregation get on their knees during worship, but getting on your knees before God serves as both adoration and humility. It is a tangible, physical reminder for us each day that we worship and rely upon a God who is greater than ourselves.

In Your Own Voice

Talk to God out loud in your own voice. Hear yourself speak to God. It will help you focus.

Prayer Time

- *Pray* for the people in your life—loved ones, friends, coworkers, and those closest to you.

- *Speak* to God about the day, including any struggles or fears you have.
- *Thank* God aloud for your blessings after reading through the gratitude list you have created.
- *Confess* attitudes or behaviors that you have that are separating you from God or others.
- *Complete* your prayer time by reciting the Lord's Prayer.

Week 1

LOVING
GOD

Week 1

LOVING GOD

Just then a lawyer stood up to test Jesus. "Teacher," he said, "what must I do to inherit eternal life?" He said to him, "What is written in the law? What do you read there?" He answered, "You shall love the Lord your God with all your heart, and with all your soul, and with all your strength, and with all your mind; and your neighbor as yourself." And he said to him, "You have given the right answer; do this, and you will live."
—Luke 10:25-28

Jesus was asked many questions. They were posed by many different people with varied motives. But there may be no question that has shaped the way Christians understand love and attempt to live it out than the one we just read that appears in all three Synoptic Gospels— the question that sparked the teaching on the Greatest Commandment. Pull out your Bible and read the three different accounts (Matthew 22:34-40; Mark 12:28-34; Luke 10:25-28), and notice the similarities and subtle differences. There are two different questions asked. Jesus answers directly the question in two accounts. The motive of the asker was clearly to test Jesus in Matthew and Luke, but his intent in Mark is less evident.

In Luke, the lawyer doesn't ask what the Greatest (or First) Commandment actually *is*. He asks the personal, "What must I do to inherit eternal life?" It is a different starting point. Jesus masterfully answers his question by asking one of his own. He says, "What is written in the law?" The man gives the same answer that Jesus did in the other Gospels. "Love the Lord your God with all your heart, and with all your soul, and with all your strength, and with all your mind; and your neighbor as yourself." Jesus replies, "You have given the right answer; do this, and you will live."

Next week we will explore the lawyer's follow-up question and Jesus' answer. But this week we ask: Just *how* are we to love the Lord our God with all of our heart, soul, strength, and mind? It seems like an unachievable state of being. I mean, how in this world are we supposed to love God with that kind of fervor in everyday living? What does that even look like? It sounds like a pipe dream to most of us. Is it found in becoming so holy that we transcend to some altered, angelic state where nothing disturbs us? I doubt it. I have met some very holy people who love God, but even they couldn't sustain that kind of intention. If we are forced to conjure up a picture of someone who has done this, we might name someone like Mother Teresa. But we struggle to imagine how our own lives could reflect that kind of devotion, dedication, and focus. It's a job in itself. Yet, we long to worship and love the Divine. It's hardwired into us. This is conceivably because we inherently know what Augustine asserted, "God cares for each of us as though each were the only one."[*] Have you experienced that? If you have tasted even a bit of that truth, you will never be the same. Experiencing the magnitude of God's care and love invites response and stokes a desire to be in relationship. And often as we begin to pursue that relationship, things slowly get in the way. While we ought to be loving the Lover with everything we have, we often

---

[*] Augustine, *Confessions*, trans. Henry Chadwick (Oxford: Oxford University Press, 2009), Book 3.11.19.

fall short. We get forgetful, distracted, and self-reliant. And God never seems to force God-self upon us.

Life Seasons

The journey of following Jesus Christ includes wandering and finding, ups and downs. There are the ebbs and flows to everyday living; we all go through seasons when we feel more connected and less connected to God. "In sync" seasons are akin to serenely floating on the water, allowing the currents to gently move us down the river of life. These seasons can also be fast-paced and in constant flow, while we enjoy the exhilarating ride and easy navigation. Taking in the beauty and blessings around us, we are grateful to God for all that is. These "in sync" seasons are balanced with periods of doubt, wandering, struggle, dryness, and/or disengagement.

Then there are those seasons when we are navigating rapids, being tossed and thrown about, trying to avoid the rocks, and doing everything we can not to capsize. And sometimes we tip over and are swimming mightily to get to safety. Strong forces and indirect currents conspire to draw us away from love and are woven into the fabric of our culture and lives—no matter the season. They affect us sometimes suddenly—sometimes slowly—but they can certainly lead us from creating the space needed to deliberately cultivate our intentional love for God.

When we are drawn away, we can convince ourselves that we don't have time, or we less deliberately just fall out of the rhythm of prioritizing God. We either don't think much about making time, or we are just plain unwilling to carve it out. We question the costs versus benefits and are too unsure of the outcomes to truly invest. Doubts creep in. We wonder if our efforts in the spiritual life actually matter. Are they leading to lives that are more beautiful and purposeful? When church participation and disciplines fall into being rote and obligatory, our connection to God and the church erodes. Combine that with a world that feels out of control, political polarization, discord in the church, and struggles in our own families, and our attention to our love for God wanes.

This can happen at any time—whether life is serene, choppy, or has high-level rapids—but the good news is that in every season there is also opportunity to rely on and deepen our love for God by continuing to engage in disciplines that keep us connected to God and the church.

Some of us have seasons in which it is more challenging to focus on our relationship with God. See if you can identify the season you currently are experiencing in the descriptions below.

Seasons of Plenty

Seasons of plenty and successful periods are wonderful. They offer comforts and opportunities. However, for some people, this season pulls them away from focusing on loving God. A pitfall of abundance is that it can deceive us into believing that we are responsible for it, which makes us operate like we have little need for God. Deuteronomy 8 says, "Don't think to yourself, My own strength and abilities have produced all this prosperity for me. Remember the Lord your God! He's the one who gives you the strength to be prosperous" (vv. 17-18 CEB). Success can gradually, unfortunately, move our hearts away from God. Often it takes unanticipated circumstances we can't control to jolt us back.

Embarking on homeownership was an exciting journey for my wife, Caroline, and me. Our lives were going through many positive changes. In addition to buying a house, we were newly married, had both recently started new jobs, and had just brought home a second dog. We were connecting with a new church and taking steps to be involved. In summary, we were busy with the blessings of life. And as a result, my spiritual practices took a back seat. To say the house we purchased needed work was an understatement. You walked in it and smelled the fresh aroma of mildew mixed with dog and cat urine. The air conditioner repairman said the ductwork was the worst he had ever seen. So Caroline and I got busy—with our time and our pocketbooks. We spent so much time in home improvement stores that I began to get to know the managers and workers. And over the course of two to three years, the house was transformed. We created a nest that was comfortable and felt like home. I actually can't even imagine the number of hours we spent on it. The summer after completing this huge renovation we went to North Carolina for a week. Caroline was five months pregnant with our first child—another blessing. During the time away, I was reading a number of books, as well as the Bible. And for whatever reason, a particular passage kept popping up—in my reading, on the radio, and so on. I thought nothing of it. But in the near future, it would have significance. The day before we were to leave, I felt a strong inclination that we had to go home. I didn't even know why.

After the ten-hour journey back to Florida, I was the first to enter the house. Caroline and the dogs were still outside. I'll never forget the noise—it was deafening. It sounded like a spraying fire hose. I walked into the kitchen and water was pouring from the ceiling like a sprinkler. I was confused since all of our pipes were under our one-story house. What I quickly discovered was the plastic icemaker line connected to the refrigerator had broken, creating a geyser of water that was shooting against the ceiling. Later we discovered that the water was likely gushing for five days. Let's just say that our newly renovated house needed some more renovating.

And like a flash, the Scripture that kept popping up now suddenly had new meaning:

> *"Do not store up for yourselves treasures on earth,*
> *where moth and rust consume and where thieves break*
> *in and steal; but store up for yourselves treasures in*
> *heaven, where neither moth nor rust consumes and*
> *where thieves do not break in and steal. For where*
> *your treasure is, there your heart will be also."*
> —*Matthew 6:19-21*

Strangely, I simultaneously experienced a deep sense of conviction and a profound sense of peace. The conviction came from the knowledge that I had spent the better part of two years being way too preoccupied with the house. It sucked up my weekends, thoughts, energy, time, and attention. While I was still engaged in my faith journey, the reality was that loving God and neighbor took a back seat. It was time that I would never get back. While it was not necessarily wrong to do renovations and repairs, some of which were necessary, the investment had been too great and the returns too small. My heart needed to be invested elsewhere.

The immediate peace I experienced came from the insight that all of this "stuff" wasn't important, and that it was all replaceable. In the big scheme of things, it wasn't that big of a deal. By God's grace, it was easy to put all of it into perspective. It truly was a spiritual awakening that happened in that moment. I was excited and invigorated, and I rushed to share my revelation with Caroline about the Scripture and how everything was going to be alright.... which was a mistake. (It's probably best to give your pregnant wife time to process water gushing from the ceiling before praising it.) We laugh about that day now, and though I wish that I could tell you that I was never again distracted from loving God during times of plenty, I can at least tell you that we remember this day and try our best to let it serve as a lesson.

Reflect upon a high season in your life, when there was abundance and you were acutely aware of blessings. Was it a time that led you to more deeply love God, or did it slowly pull you away? How can a season of plenty guide your actions to love God?

Seasons of Difficulty

Times of difficulty—just like abundance—can bring us closer to God or drive a wedge between us and God. They can affect our ability (or willingness) to love God. Scarcity, debilitating suffering, and conditions we can't control not only bring about perplexing questions but also can leave us feeling empty and alone. If the pain doesn't drive us toward God and community, we often allow it to separate us from the same. It may be that we just don't know what or how to pray. Or we may not be able to see how any good can come out of the tumultuous storm we are navigating. Have you ever been there? When in the darkness, Paul's wisdom in the Letter to the Thessalonians makes no sense at all:

"Pray without ceasing, give thanks in all circumstances; for this is the will of God in Christ Jesus for you" (1 Thessalonians 5:17-18).

Early on in my walk with Christ, I was struggling. Things were hard, and I had a multitude of challenges to navigate, most of which I created through my own brokenness (but not all of them). Asking God or anyone else for help was not something to which I was accustomed. I didn't have much experience because I was used to managing life on my own terms: stuffing, avoiding, or denying my need. I could put on the "Sunday smiles" with the best of them—you know, when you are walking around with pain in your gut at church but are smiling away when people ask how your life is. I thought that I should be able to handle it without assistance. Pain and fear broke down my unwillingness. It was only in a vulnerable moment that I relented to my resistance and contacted a trusted mentor for advice.

The man was wise, brutally honest, and direct. His demeanor, delivery, and presence were comforting yet didn't sugarcoat any difficult truths. After detailing my situation, he said that my way of dealing with life wasn't working and that a new attitude would be required for change. He said, "Your tank is empty. You must take a new approach that shifts reliance away from your own resources to God's. Trust more fully in God's love." His advice and proclamations were underwhelming. But, again, I was willing to explore more of what that meant, if only because I was in so much discomfort. Pain can be either a stumbling block or motivator for growth. I bit on the suggestion. "Okay, so how? How do I have a new attitude, and what does the approach look like?" He didn't answer directly, responding with, "I monitor the level of my car's fuel tank closely. I never let it get below the halfway mark, ever. Whenever it approaches half, I beeline it to a filling station and fill it up." The puzzled look on my face must have spoken volumes. So he continued, "You see, there are always times in life when we face difficulties, when we have to travel much farther than we thought without the benefit of a filling station. If I make sure I always fill up before it goes to half a tank, I can be sure that I have done everything possible to not run out of gas."

Again, my scrunched face must have communicated what I was thinking, which was, "What are you talking about? Fill our tank up with what? What does filling your gas tank have to do with anything?" I truly just did not get it. He finally explained (and the lightbulb in my brain finally lit) that *turning to God* is what fills the tank, and we need to go to the filling station habitually. As Christians, we do that through prayer, contemplative practices (meditation), and reading and reflecting upon the Scripture and worship. These are the vehicles through which our tank is filled. And regularly going to the station for a top off ensures that when difficult times come, we have enough to keep going. In other words, going to and cultivating our relationship with God is best done methodically through spiritual practices. Through them we are filled, and our obedience to them illustrates our love for God and desire to grow.

My mentor ended with a word of warning. He said, "It's hard to play catch-up when your tank has been running on fumes for a long time. If you run into a desert on 'empty,' you'll probably be stranded for a while."

What is the current level in your tank? How often are you visiting the filling station? Is it easier for you to connect to God in difficulty, or is it the time when you shy away? What does going to God in difficult times to fill your tank look like? Which spiritual disciplines connect you to God the most?

"Ordinary Time"

If you grew up in or currently worship in a mainline Protestant or Catholic tradition, then you are likely familiar with the liturgical calendar. Though it varies slightly among denominations, its purpose is for Christians to reflect upon, celebrate, and engage the mystery of Christ intentionally throughout the liturgical year, which is divided into a number of "seasons." Each one commences with the anticipation of another. Advent is the first season, usually falling in late November or early December, and begins on the fourth Sunday that precedes

Christmas. Some other seasons are Christmas, Epiphany, Lent, Easter, and Pentecost. These seasons commemorate the highs and lows of Christ's story, including the birth of Jesus, the first recognition of Jesus as Christ, the journey to the cross, God raising Jesus from the dead, and the powerful coming of the Holy Spirit that started the church. But the liturgical calendar also includes another very important season called Ordinary Time. It's the longest season of the year and takes us through the life of Jesus. "Ordinary" isn't meant to denote rote or boring; it is designed to bring about growth and maturity.*

Like the calendar, the largest part of our lives resides in ordinary time. Things are chugging along. The rhythms of life are on rinse and repeat. And while lots of maturity and growth in love can materialize from apexes and the nadirs, there is a special opportunity to cultivate loving God in the simple, in the repeatable, in the mundane.

But just like in times of plenty and difficulty, ordinary time has its challenges.

Many of my Protestant peers have discovered the fruit of spending time at Catholic monasteries, and I regularly spend time in one myself. It is a holy place for me. It was there that I responded more fully to my call and discovered ancient contemplative practices that I now apply regularly in my life. I still make the pilgrimage every eighteen months or so to disconnect, recharge, and connect with God. After one of my trips, when our kids were young, I was sharing with my wife the experience and suggestions that the monks offered to dive deeper into a life of contemplation. I had already established a daily practice of silence and was trying to increase it, and I told her of one monk who strongly asserted that centering prayer should be done twice a day, with each prayer period being twenty minutes. Caroline literally laughed out loud, and said, "I'd like for him to come and live at our house for a couple of weeks to see if he could manage the household, two little kids, and two twenty-minute periods of meditation. Have you ever noticed it is always single men who have never had children who

---

* "Ordinary Time," United States Conference of Catholic Bishops, http://www.usccb.org /prayer-and-worship/liturgical-year/ordinary-time.cfm, accessed August 20, 2018.

assert these things?" While I had returned rejuvenated, my wife was alone dealing with middle-of-the-night feedings, diaper changes, more feedings, baths, and the persistent needs of little kids. Her only refuge was in the bathroom—and even there she couldn't escape! Even with a partner, this kind of "ordinary" understandably wears down parents.

No matter what life stage you are in, whether you are single, married, divorced, caring for aging parents, or in the twilight of life, days can begin to run together, and the weeks fly by. Everything can feel downright monotonous and so can loving God. But we must find ways to love God in the cadences of everyday life, and living in the ordinary ensures we will love more in the way Jesus commands. If we don't, a robust love for God and spiritual life won't be manifested.

After reflecting upon the different seasons, which would you say that you are in? In which season is it hardest to express your love for God? How can you love God in times of plenty, during difficulties, and in the ordinary?

One way to answer is to ask another question: If I wanted to cultivate a more meaningful relationship with someone, how would I do it? It's not rocket science. You'd spend more time with them, you'd be more intentional in getting to know who they are, you'd make sacrifices for them, and you'd be more and more vulnerable with your strengths and struggles. To grow the relationship, there must be commitment, encouragement, and accountability. In other words, engage in the activities and actions that cultivate the relationship. Why would a relationship with God be any different?

The Key

In his classic work *The Art of Loving*, Erich Fromm[*] says that love is not a feeling, but a practice. Love isn't a feeling? I would say it isn't *only* a feeling, but a direction of the will. It is a decision. If we are to love God with all of our heart, mind, soul, and strength, our *faithfulness to spiritual practices is the key*. It always has been. If you

---

[*] See Erich Fromm, *The Art of Loving* (New York: Harper & Row, 1956).

look at the people who have devotedly tried to live out the Greatest Commandment in their lives, you most often find that they are part of a faith community, and that they have been obedient to the time-tested spiritual disciplines. Living out loving God with all that we have and all of who we are necessitates that we do it over the long haul.

For a number of years, I had the honor of serving my church by working with a group to identify, develop, and deploy leaders who would be charged with connecting people to deeper relationship with God through spiritual practices. It should come as no surprise that the names that rose to the surface were of people noticed first because of their engagement in church. People who came to worship, engaged in small groups, and served got on the group's radar. While these are not always iron-clad predictors of whether people have leadership gifts or if they are loving God with all that they have, we all intuitively knew that people who regularly engaged in spiritual practices were people who were more likely to be growing in love for God and neighbor.

Before diving into the "business" of the meeting, the group would sit in silent contemplation for two to three minutes. Then, each person would share prayer requests and then check in about their spiritual life. Specifically, they would respond to questions about the ways in which they were nurturing their relationship with God through praying, reading, and reflecting on Scripture, and participating in worship. Again, this leadership group comprised high-capacity and faithful leaders, dedicated to Jesus and the church. And what I found is that most everyone felt like they were falling short at one time or another.

So if you feel like you are falling short, you are not alone. Some people are too hard on themselves (and others aren't hard enough). Most of us recognize how challenging it is to live out this love for God consistently in everyday life. The very realization that we fall short can connect us more deeply to our need for God's grace found in Jesus Christ. This isn't meant to be a guilt trip, nor should it let us off the hook. In fact, if the condemning and critical voices in your head are keeping you stuck, either by preventing you from starting anew or by suggesting that you don't need to, I suspect that that messaging doesn't come from God.

God takes us exactly as we are. Our failures do not prevent God from loving us. That's the beauty of God's love. And it is the knowledge of that love that ignites us to love God back. God takes us where we are, but doesn't want to leave us there! Loving God should be about progress, not perfection, although any progress made is usually never steady up and to the right. Begin again, no matter how many times you have stalled or stumbled. Because the truth is, we are all stumbling toward the Light. And it is best to stumble together. Community helps us remember the Light, directs our lives toward the Light, and encourages us to trust the Light. Jesus said, "I am the light of the world. Whoever follows me will never walk in darkness but will have the light of life" (John 8:12).

How can we love God in times of plenty, in times of difficulty, and in ordinary times? There are a few simple steps that will get us started:

1. Acknowledge what season you are in.
2. Analyze what is getting in the way of our focusing on the love of God.
3. Seek to know and experience God through spiritual practices.

Psalm 36:9 says, "With you is the fountain of life; in your light we see light." Our actions, our efforts to determine what season we are in, the way we analyze obstacles, and our commitment to spiritual practices are important ways to live love. An encouraging word to remember is that God's grace empowers and strengthens us, because we can't do any of this on our own!

John Wesley, the founder of the Methodist movement, believed that spiritual practices are the way that God works in us, confirming our faith and growing us in love. He called them the means of grace.*
In our congregation, we point to seven spiritual practices in which disciples should engage to grow in belief and action, which grows their love for God and neighbor. They are prayer and meditation, Scripture reflection, worship, financial generosity, sharing our faith, serving, and

---

* "The Wesleyan Means of Grace," The United Methodist Church, http://www.umc.org/how
  -we-serve/the-wesleyan-means-of-grace, accessed August 20, 2018.

small group community.* They take many shapes and forms, but all act as glue that binds us to God. We will focus on three for this study: worship, prayer, and Scripture reflection. These will direct us to the filling station and enable us to express our love for God no matter our current season of life.

Worship with God as Your Audience

I was captivated by the music of the 1980s and 1990s. Songs could be heard blasting from my room, on my Walkman, and out of my boom box. I had vinyl albums and cassette tapes. Lyrics from rock and roll, thoughts of rock star hair, and the sounds of emerging grunge bands filled my head.

Nirvana's hit album *Nevermind*† was a favorite. The opening track, "Smells Like Teen Spirit," has been listed as one of the greatest songs of all time. A line from that song perfectly summarizes the spirit with which I came to worship in those early years after recommitting to Christ: "Here we are now, entertain us!"‡

I spent years going to worship with an expectation of receiving something. I wanted worship to fill my tank. Every once in a while I hear that sentiment in comments from people. "I got so much out of worship today!" or "I didn't get anything out of worship today. I just wasn't fed." When we enter into worship with that expectation, we have been clouded by our consumer-based mentality—focusing on our own preferences of what we like and don't like. Now I hope that your faith community creates worship experiences full of inspiration, with excellent music and transformational Bible teaching. Those are all important to sustain us and help along our journey. But there is more to worship.

Danish theologian Søren Kierkegaard pronounced the folly in that perspective and offered a transformational metaphor that changes the way people understand worship. He says when we go to worship, we

---

* See James A. Harnish and Justin LaRosa, *A Disciple's Path* (Nashville: Abingdon Press, 2012).

† Nirvana, *Nevermind*, DGC Records, 1991.

‡ Nirvana, "Smells Like Teen Spirit," by Kurt Cobain, Krist Novoselic, and Dave Grohl, track 1 on *Nevermind*, DGC Records, 1991, compact disc.

tend to think of the sanctuary as the theater. The people on stage who are leading worship serve as the actors and performers. The director is God, who is off-stage. And finally, the audience in the theater seats or pews are the receivers.

But Kierkegaard flips this on its head by asserting that the people on the stage are not the performers but the *directors*. They are directing the people out in the pews to *perform*. The songs of praise, prayers, confession, and offering are directed to the audience. And that *audience is God*.[*]

We gather in worship to be present to God, to be grateful, and to worship. Worshiping in Christian community helps us remember who God is, to remember who we are, and to remember who we are called to be—no matter whether we are in seasons of plenty, difficulty, or ordinary times. Centering ourselves on remembering—no matter what's going on in our lives—realigns our hearts toward God. As we connect with gratitude, we can more fully worship. The movement of our hearts pivots from watching worship to participating in it. And as we worship rooted and grounded in that intention, we more fully love with all of our hearts, minds, soul, and strength.

Does this shift the way you think about preparing for and entering into worship? How will you prepare differently for worship this week?

Pray Knowing God Is Present

When the Bible records Jesus praying, he often went off alone.[†] Incorporating prayer in worship and with others is a fruitful practice, but going to God alone is an essential ingredient for any disciple who desires to live out the Greatest Commandment. It doesn't have to be on the side of a mountain or in a spiritual place. It can be anywhere and everywhere.

Imagine never talking with or listening to your spouse or significant other—how close would your relationship be? John Wesley said in a

---

[*] See Søren Kierkegaard, *Purity of Heart Is to Will One Thing*, trans. Douglas Steere (New York: Harper and Brothers, 1948).

[†] See Matthew 14:23; 26:36, Mark 1:35; Luke 5:16; 6:12.

pastoral address that we "may as well expect a child to grow without food, as a soul to grow without private prayer."*

Yet, some of us are frustrated by prayer. We don't know what to pray for. Or if we do, moments after we start, we realize that we have been thinking about lunch, the laundry, or what we are going to do later. This can make us wonder if it is making any difference at all. I wrote a portion of this book at coffee shops. When trying to concentrate on the task at hand, I found myself being distracted by all the different conversations and movement around me. Just like the coffee shop, there is a lot of noise and movement inside our head when we pray. The incessant mental chatter can be loud, distracting, or even critical. But don't fret; it's a normal part of the human condition and something that challenges everyone.

Perhaps the difficulty is lessened when we release the belief we are separate. The Cistercian monk Thomas Keating said, "The chief thing that separates us from God is the thought that we are separated from [God]. If we get rid of that thought, our troubles will be greatly reduced."† This applies to prayer. You aren't separated from God. If you are willing to believe it, prayer becomes easier. German theologian Meister Eckhart expressed the same sentiment this way, "I am as sure as I live that nothing is so near to me as God. God is nearer to me than I am to myself; my existence depends on the nearness and the presence of God."‡

God is present when we pray. Jesus' instructions for prayer are in Matthew 6. It lists what to do and not do in prayer, assuring us that God knows what we need before we ask, and it gives us the Lord's Prayer. God knows our hearts, feelings, needs, and sins. Prayer often seems like a one-way conversation in which we are talking to God. But like any relationship, in addition to talking, we should also listen.

---

* Luke Tyerman, *The Life and Times of the Rev. John Wesley, M. A., Founder of the Methodists*, Volume II (London: Hodder and Stoughton, 1870), 515, https://archive.org/details/lifetimesofjohnw02tyeruoft/page/514.

† Thomas Keating, *Open Mind, Open Heart* (New York: Continuum, 2002), 44, https://books.google.com/books?id=pINxHWGTa6EC&printsec=frontcover#v=onepage&q&f=false.

‡ *Meister Eckhart's Sermons*, trans. Claud Field (London: H. R. Allenson, 1909), 19–20.

And there are forms of prayer and reading the Scripture that open us up to noticing God in the present moment. Because prayer isn't just about saying words and thoughts. Those are important ways that we commune with God. But prayer can be expanded to resting in God's presence, centering ourselves in the naked moment, where God is most available to us—the now. Franciscan priest Richard Rohr avows, "Prayer is not primarily saying words or thinking thoughts. It is, rather, a stance. It's a way of living *in* the Presence, living in *awareness* of the Presence, and even of enjoying the Presence. The full contemplative is not just aware of the Presence, but trusts, allows, and delights in it."*

Read the Bible, and Let the Bible Read You

St. Jerome, the theologian and saint from the fourth and fifth centuries, said, "Ignorance of Scripture is ignorance of Christ."† Ouch. That should echo in our souls. It is a powerful if not unsettling proclamation. Even if his assertion is half true, it should ignite a fire within us to study the Bible and reflect upon the mysteries of our foundational texts.

The Bible reveals through the story of God's relationship with God's people. God is most fully revealed in and through the life, death, and resurrection of Jesus Christ. To not crack it open (or open it on our devices), wrestle with it, or allow it to form us is to miss out on deeply knowing the character and love of God.

So there are two simple tasks:

1. Read and study the Bible.
2. Let the Bible read you.

---

* Richard Rohr, *Everything Belongs: The Gift of Contemplative Prayer*, Revised and Updated Edition (New York: Crossroad, 2003), 31, https://www.amazon.com/dp/B011H5IDJG /ref=dp-kindle-redirect?_encoding=UTF8&btkr=1#reader_B011H5IDJG.

† ZENIT Staff, "Pope Affirms 'Ignorance of Scripture Is Ignorance of Christ.'" ZENIT, June 19, 2015, https://zenit.org/articles/pope-affirms-ignorance-of-scripture-is-ignorance-of-christ/, accessed August 20, 2018.

Shortly after recommitting my life to Jesus Christ, I truly had a desire to learn more about God. Before then, I wasn't shy about criticizing the Bible. The irony was that I had never really spent much time reading it. When I decided to actually explore it, I thought the best way would be to start at the beginning and read it book by book, like you would any other book. Boy, was I wrong! It wasn't long before I discovered the challenge and brutality of that task. I didn't understand any context. I barely made it through the first five books before getting discouraged and unmotivated. It wasn't until someone suggested I start in the Gospels (and also process it with others) that I began to understand this sacred and confusing book.

John Wesley said that the Bible was twice inspired, once when written and once when read.* Reading the Scriptures opens our hearts, minds, and souls to God. Learning the context of the passages will help us understand more about the history, the people, and the authors. More important, we come to know God as a benevolent and loving Creator, Redeemer, and Sustainer. This resource is not a Bible study. If you are new to the faith or are uncomfortable with the Bible, plan to study it with a group of people in your congregation.

I listed a second task that differs from the first: allow the Bible to read you. How is that done? St. Benedict said to listen and "incline the ear of thy heart."† We incline the ears of our hearts by getting out of the driver's seat. We allow The Spirit to whisper to us through a reflective reading of the text, which cultivates our ability to listen and respond to God's word. Christians have been doing this for centuries through the ancient practice called *Lectio Divina*, which means "Divine Reading." Unlike Bible study, *Lectio Divina* is a way of being in conversation with Jesus Christ and allowing him to suggest the topic of conversation through the passage we are reading.

* F. Belton Joyner Jr., *United Methodist Questions, United Methodist Answers: Exploring Christian Faith* (Louisville: Westminster John Knox Press, 2007), 65.

† Saint Benedict, Abbot of Monte Cassino, *The Holy Rule of St. Benedict: The 1949 Edition*, electronic text trans. by Boniface Verheyen (Grand Rapids, MI: Christian Classics Ethereal Library, 1949), 2, http://www.documentacatholicaomnia.eu/03d/0480-0547,_Benedictus_Nursinus,_Regola,_EN.pdf.

There are generally four movements in *Lectio Divina*, and they are detailed in the appendix on page 141. But here's the gist: Take a short passage of Scripture, no more than a few verses. *Read* it very slowly. Then read it again, repeating and reflecting upon it. Let the words sink down into you. Do this until a word strikes you from the passage. That is your word from God and is to be carried with you throughout your day. *Reflect* on the word by thinking about why it might have been given to you and talk to God about it. Then, *respond* to God by talking to God about the word or phrase you received. Lastly, rest with God in silence. When your mind wanders, use the word to center yourself. You read, God prompts, you reflect, you respond, and then you rest in God. That word can go with us all throughout the day.

Augustine is commonly quoted as saying, "To fall in love with God is the greatest romance; to seek him the greatest adventure; to find him, the greatest human achievement."[*]

It is good to remember our simple but effective path: faithful, fruitful, and surrendered. Practicing the spiritual practices of worshiping, praying, and reflecting on the Bible is a great adventure! In it and through it, we will fall in love!

---

[*] "St. Augustine of Hippo: Quotes from Augustine of Hippo," Our Lady of Mercy, http://olmlaycarmelites.org/quote/augustine, accessed November 15, 2018.

─ Week 1 ─
DEVOTIONALS

Day 1: Gutter Cleaning

Scripture

> *Create in me a clean heart, O God,*
> *and put a new and right spirit within me.*
> *—Psalm 51:10*

No matter the season, I have to be vigilant attending to the gutters on my house. They are always filling up. The three oaks in my yard deluge them with leaves, twigs, pollen, and dirt, which become particularly robust in the fall and spring. My reminder to clean them in any season comes in the form of rain. Instead of draining the normal way through the downspout, water dumps over the edges in a number of locations because it has nowhere else to go. And when I see evidence that it's time to clean them again, I dread it. Cleaning those gutters is my least favorite house chore.

After a few years of frequently being on the step ladder and roof, I decided to invest in gutter-guards (I am a slow learner), which essentially sit on the gutters and stop leaves from filling them up while still allowing water to pass through. This made things better, but didn't entirely eliminate the problem, as the gunk eventually just sat on top of the guards, clogging up the little holes that were supposed to allow the water to get to the gutters. And eventually I found myself back on the step ladder, not only wiping the top of the guards, but then taking them off and scooping out the smelly, decaying material that had made its way through the holes.

Relating this to our relationship with God, the gutters serve to keep God's love flowing in our lives—directed toward loving God and neighbor. The gutter guards, when secured in place, limit the debris that gets caught in there. An encouraging faith community and regularly attending to spiritual practices serve as our gutter guards to keep the love flowing. They don't keep everything out, but they certainly can reduce the muck. The material that builds up is sin in all its forms, blocking the flow.

Take a moment to reflect upon what is blocking you from intentionally loving God. Psalm 51 is the contrite psalm where David is most likely confessing grievous acts of adultery and murder. He begs for forgiveness and prays for God to create a new heart in him. He's asking God to clean out his gutter. Even though we may not have those particular sins, we have need before God. Our gutters need cleaning so the love can flow freely again.

Reflection Questions

- What is cluttering your life and needs to be extracted?
- Where are your blocks?
- Are there things that you are holding on to?
- What can you confess to God and ask forgiveness for?

Prayer

God of power, create in me a clean heart. I confess that there are things that are blocking me from a fuller love (name them). Please forgive me. Give me the discernment to know how to best remove the buildup and to best utilize the gutter guards in my spiritual life.

Thank you God for your call to love those who persecute, and for the way it gives us a picture into your extravagant grace. Amen.

Challenge

To confess the blockages in your life to loving God. Invite God to remove any debris that inhibits you from loving God more fully.

Day 2: Attitude of Gratitude

Scripture

> *Rejoice in the Lord always; again I will say, Rejoice.*
> *Let your gentleness be known to everyone. The Lord is*
> *near. Do not worry about anything, but in everything*
> *by prayer and supplication with thanksgiving let your*
> *requests be made known to God. And the peace of*
> *God, which surpasses all understanding, will guard*
> *your hearts and your minds in Christ Jesus.*
> *—Philippians 4:4-7*

His eyes lit the room and his smile projected friendliness. From the first time I met him, he exuded gratitude. It seeped and oozed. It wasn't faked, forced or disingenuous. Honestly, I initially found him very annoying—mostly because I was in one of the most difficult seasons of my life and fairly miserable. But he was one of those people that had that magnetism about him. You wanted to be around him. Along with gratitude, he radiated joy, gentleness, and non-judgment. I wondered how he did it. So I asked. He didn't have a profound answer. I would come to learn that not everything in his life was comfortable, secure, or perfect. He had wreckage from his past and current struggles too. But, he didn't try to distort or twist reality to ignore the pain in his life or the world's. He wasn't whistling in the dark—he was deeply connected to God's grace. He said that life had taught him to surrender to the circumstances around him and be grateful to God no matter what. Because of that grace, he lived differently. He, better than most, could be thankful for what was, what is, and what was to come. He had an attitude of gratitude—and I wanted what he had.

Today, live your life with an attitude of gratitude. Read the Scripture again and then review your gratitude list.

Reflection Questions

- What is the area currently in your life for which you are not grateful?

- Think about a mental preoccupation that swirls around the negative. Is there something to discover about it, around it, or in it for which you give thanks to God?
- What are the worries that you have? Bring them to God and ask for peace.
- How can you bring awareness to your blessings all throughout the day?

Prayer

God, help me connect to my life as a gift and open my eyes to ways to be a living gift to others. Amen.

Challenge

To practice an attitude of gratitude.

Day 3: Be Still

Scripture 1

> *"And whenever you pray, do not be like the hypocrites; for they love to stand and pray in the synagogues and at the street corners, so that they may be seen by others. Truly I tell you, they have received their reward. But whenever you pray, go into your room and shut the door and pray to your Father who is in secret; and your Father who sees in secret will reward you."*
> —*Matthew 6:5-6*

Scripture 2

> *"Be still, and know that I am God!"*
> —*Psalm 46:10*

I suspect that the desire to be quiet, still, and center on the present moment is from God. The present moment is the place where God is most present and accessible to us, but where we spend the least time.

Our thoughts are consumed with what already has happened (past) or what will happen (future)—and rarely with what is happening *now*.

But when we try to get still, our minds batter us with a constant stream of thoughts, reflections, commentaries, and judgments. Maybe that's why meditation, mindfulness, and yoga are so popular in our time. In recent years, the benefits of practicing these disciplines have been researched, studied, and documented. About twenty-five years ago, I couldn't shut off my mind. Repetitive thoughts were affecting my sleep, mood, and life. When I would attempt to go to sleep, thoughts would bounce from one thing to another—relentlessly. Out of necessity, I explored Eastern traditions of meditation, not knowing that there was a rich tradition of silence in Christianity. Even today, many Christians who seek out meditation are blissfully unaware of Christianity's centuries-old meditative tradition called contemplation. Many of the benefits are the same: calmer mind, stress reduction, and better focus. But that's not the point in contemplative practices like centering prayer and *Lectio Divina*. The intention is to grow and deepen our relationship with Jesus Christ through silence and attending to the Presence of God.

Jesus' teaching on prayer is found in the Sermon on the Mount. Many early Christians point to this passage as one that invites disciples to pray in silence. Jesus is directing this teaching to the disciples. He tells them not to be hypocrites who pray so that others can see how holy they are. That kind of motivation isn't about loving God. Jesus tells them to go into their inner room and close the door. This is where it gets interesting. Not all translations have an inner room. Some have a closet, some have an inner chamber, and some just call it a room. Later in Matthew 8, Jesus says, "Foxes have holes, and birds of the air have nests; but the Son of Man has nowhere to lay his head" (v. 20). Jesus and the disciples don't exactly have a place to live, a home in which to close the door. Because of this, some early Christians thought that perhaps Jesus was talking about going into the inner room of your heart. And that to close the door meant that the disciples were to detach from the faculties that make the mind race during prayer (will, intellect, imagination, and memory). Sounds like a tall order. But there is a way to quell the noise and cultivate your relationship with Christ.

Thomas Merton describes it this way:

> In the "prayer of the heart" we seek first of all the deepest ground of our identity in God. We do not reason about dogmas of faith, or "the mysteries." We seek rather to gain a direct existential grasp, a personal experience of the deepest truths of life and faith, *finding ourselves in God's truth.* . . . *Prayer* then means yearning for the simple presence of God, for a personal understanding of [God's] word, for knowledge of [God's] will and for capacity to hear and obey [God].*

If you have ever had difficulty focusing during prayer, you are not alone. But the psalmist promises if we are still we will experience God. It doesn't always feel like we are experiencing God in silence because life is so busy. Even after practicing silence for a very long time, my mind can still be firing rapidly, noisy, and overactive. But it's okay. Creating interior stillness takes time, regular practice, and a method. The intention of praying to God in silence even when the mind is busy is loving God with all of our heart, mind, soul, and strength. In stillness, we will know.

Today during your prayer and Scripture time, rest in God through the practice of centering prayer (see Appendix A).

Reflection Questions

- When you are quiet, what does your thought world gravitate toward?
- Are the voices kind? Critical? Distracting?
- Can you detach from those thoughts and gently return to your centering word?
- How can you bring stillness throughout your day?

---

* Thomas Merton, *Contemplative Prayer* (New York: Doubleday, 1996), 67.

Prayer

God, I offer all of myself to you, my thoughts, my heart, my impurities, all to you. Be with me in the silence. Amen.

Challenge

To practice silence as a way of resting in God.

Day 4: Letting God Read Us

Scripture

> *O LORD, you have searched me and known me.*
> *You know when I sit down and when I rise up;*
>   *you discern my thoughts from far away.*
> *You search out my path and my lying down,*
>   *and are acquainted with all my ways.*
> *Even before a word is on my tongue,*
>   *O LORD, you know it completely.*
> *You hem me in, behind and before,*
>   *and lay your hand upon me.*
> *Such knowledge is too wonderful for me;*
>   *it is so high that I cannot attain it.*
>   *—Psalm 139:1-6*

Karl Rahner, the influential Jesuit, said, "The devout Christian of the future will either be a 'mystic,' one who has experienced 'something,' or he will cease to be anything at all."* The quotation points to the difference of a person knowing *about* God and *knowing* God.

Who is the person who knows you best? For me, it is my wife. She can read me like a book. Her intuition about what's going on in my mind and heart is spot-on, sometimes when I don't even see it myself.

---

* Karl Rahner, "Christian Living Formerly and Today," *Theological Investigations* 7, trans. David Bourke (New York: Herder & Herder, 1971), 15, quoted in Harvey D. Egan, "The Mystical Theology of Karl Rahner," *The Way* 52, no. 2 (April 2013): 51.

God's knowing of us surpasses our understanding. This mind-blowing thought is difficult to grasp. And the Bible can reveal God's knowledge of us and connect us to God in a deeper way.

Reading the Bible for understanding and knowledge is critical to faith. We come to learn about God, Jesus' life, death, and resurrection, and how our story fits into it all. We learn about the doctrines and concepts. These are important. But letting the Bible read us is an effective way for us to experience God more personally and intimately.

Wherever you are, close your eyes and imagine that you are sitting down with God during your devotional time. And instead of you beginning the conversation, allow God to begin. What would God say? It's an interesting thought exercise, but we can actually practice it. The practice of *Lectio Divina* is all about letting God suggest the topics of conversation and reflection. We slowly read the Bible, and then, we allow it to read us. Christ suggests the conversation topics through a word or a phrase. It is a surrendering of sorts, a deeper kind of listening, since we aren't controlling the process.

As we cultivate the practice of letting the Bible read us, we begin to experience God in a deeper and more meaningful way. God's love becomes more real to us. And we will not only know more *about* God but also *know* God.

Reflection Questions

- Who is the person who can read you like a book?
- How is God speaking to you today through God's word?

Prayer

God, I give thanks for your Word. You know me better than I know myself. Open my mind and heart to the way you want to speak to me through the Bible. Amen.

Challenge

To let the Bible read you through *Lectio Divina*.

Day 5: Creation

Scripture

> *Heaven is declaring God's glory;*
> *the sky is proclaiming his handiwork.*
> *One day gushes the news to the next,*
> *and one night informs another what needs to be*
> *known.*
> *Of course, there's no speech, no words—*
> *their voices can't be heard—*
> *but their sound extends throughout the world;*
> *their words reach the ends of the earth.*
>
> *God has made a tent in heaven for the sun.*
> *The sun is like a groom*
> *coming out of his honeymoon suite;*
> *like a warrior, it thrills at running its course.*
> *It rises in one end of the sky;*
> *its circuit is complete at the other.*
> *Nothing escapes its heat.*
>
> *—Psalm 19:1-6 CEB*

French philosopher Simone Weil once said, "The beauty of the world is Christ's tender smile for us coming through matter."* I went on my first camping trip when I was nine years old in the sticks of central Pennsylvania. One night I couldn't sleep, so I went to sit by the fire. It was dimly lit as the last embers were quietly glowing. As I sat there in the middle of the night, by myself, I caught a glimpse of the sky out of the corner of my eye. As I gazed upward, its radiance exploded. The grandeur of the stars glowed. I was captured in awe like it is described in Psalm 8:

> *O LORD, our Sovereign,*
> *how majestic is your name in all the earth!*

---

* Simone Weil, "Love of the Order of the World," in *Waiting for God*, trans. Emma Craufurd (New York: G. P. Putnam's Sons, 1951), 164–65.

You have set your glory above the heavens. . . .

When I look at your heavens, the work of your fingers,
*   the moon and the stars that you have established;*
what are human beings that you are mindful of them,
*   mortals that you care for them?*

Yet you have made them a little lower than God,
*   and crowned them with glory and honor.*
You have given them dominion over the works of your
hands;
*   you have put all things under their feet,*
all sheep and oxen,
*   and also the beasts of the field,*
the birds of the air, and the fish of the sea,
*   whatever passes along the paths of the seas.*

O LORD, our Sovereign,
*   how majestic is your name in all the earth!*
—Psalm 8:1, 3-9

The cosmos seized me like never before. The grandeur of nature can help usher in our love for God, especially if we can connect that it is Christ's tender smile for us. Many people describe feeling connected to God in the splendor of a sunset, the power of a thunderstorm, or the stillness in the woods.

Reflection Questions

- Reflect upon a time when you have experienced a moment of majesty in nature.
- When were you overtaken by the depth of this existence, the beauty of this world, or your inability to grasp it all?

Prayer

Let the words of my mouth and the meditations of my heart be pleasing to you. Show me the way your creation proclaims your love for me and the world. Amen.

```
┌──────────────  Challenge  ──────────────┐
│   To get outside in nature and enjoy God's  │
│   creation. Go outside today and be present to │
│   God in nature. Take a walk, sit on a bench, or │
│   simply take in the beauty of your surroundings. │
└──────────────────────────────────────────┘
```

Day 6: Trust

Scripture

> But now thus says the LORD,
> he who created you, O Jacob,
> he who formed you, O Israel:
> Do not fear, for I have redeemed you;
> I have called you by name, you are mine.
> When you pass through the waters, I will be with you;
> and through the rivers, they shall not overwhelm you;
> when you walk through fire you shall not be burned,
> and the flame shall not consume you.
> —Isaiah 43:1-2

Trust forms the foundation upon which love can grow. We need it in all of our relationships. Without it, love won't grow and thrive. It is no different with God. Loving God with all of our heart, mind, soul, and strength will mean that we have to trust more. But trust not only takes time to develop, it also means that we sometimes will have to risk and give up control.

Most people hold onto control until their lives stop working. Search your thoughts for the places you have been trying to control someone or something or for the places where your life isn't working. God's invitation can be to start trusting in him more. Whether it's our finances, romances, health, or anything else, trusting that God is with us and is handling it is a step toward love. Isaiah's comforting words can help us to trust no matter the situation or the outcomes.

Reflection Questions

- Is there an area in your life where you are not fully trusting God?
- What would trusting God look like today in this situation?

Prayer

God, trusting you in the places in my life where things are going well is easy. Help me to trust that you are working in the situations that I can't control. Amen.

Challenge

To trust God today.

Day 7: Rest and Worship

Scripture

> *Shout triumphantly to the LORD, all the earth!*
> *Serve the LORD with celebration!*
> *Come before him with shouts of joy!*
> *Know that the LORD is God—*
> *he made us; we belong to him.*
> *We are his people,*
> *the sheep of his own pasture.*
> *Enter his gates with thanks;*
> *enter his courtyards with praise!*
> *Thank him! Bless his name!*
> *Because the LORD is good,*
> *his loyal love lasts forever;*
> *his faithfulness lasts generation after generation.*
> —*Psalm 100:1-5 CEB*

You have come to the last day in the week. You have been faithful to spiritual practices. You have prayed, read Scripture, remembered your blessings, talked to God in your own voice, and been in silence. You have been faithful in spending time with God. These are ways you have intentionally loved God this week. Sunday is the day we remember that we are to rest, recharge, and refuel by slowing down.

If you have not yet gone to your faith community to worship, reread the section titled "Worship with God as Your Audience." Prepare yourself for corporate worship by reminding yourself that God is the audience of the experience. Review your gratitude list, and remember that God is closer to you than you are to yourself.

Practice *Lectio Divina* with Psalm 100, and take the word God gives you, saying it throughout your day.

Prayer

Lord of all, giver of life, help me to rest today. Prepare and align my heart to worship. I come with an intention of gratitude. Remind me that I belong to you, and that your love for me is eternal. Fill me with your love and grace. As I sing, pray, hear the passages of Scripture and reflect upon them, may I worship with you being the audience. In Christ's name. Amen.

Challenge

**To rest on the sabbath and worship
with your faith community.**

Week 2
LOVING
NEIGHBOR

Week 2

LOVING NEIGHBOR

Just then a lawyer stood up to test Jesus. "Teacher," he said, "what must I do to inherit eternal life?" He said to him, "What is written in the law? What do you read there?" He answered, "You shall love the Lord your God with all your heart, and with all your soul, and with all your strength, and with all your mind; and your neighbor as yourself." And he said to him, "You have given the right answer; do this, and you will live."
—Luke 10:25-28

After Jesus tells him the Greatest Commandment, the lawyer digs deeper, as described by Luke:

But wanting to justify himself, he asked Jesus, "And who is my neighbor?" Jesus replied, "A man was going down from Jerusalem to Jericho, and fell into the hands of robbers, who stripped him, beat him, and went away, leaving him half dead. Now by chance a priest was going down that road; and when he saw him, he passed by on the other side. So likewise a

*Levite, when he came to the place and saw him, passed
by on the other side. But a Samaritan while traveling
came near him; and when he saw him, he was moved
with pity. He went to him and bandaged his wounds,
having poured oil and wine on them. Then he put him
on his own animal, brought him to an inn, and took
care of him. The next day he took out two denarii, gave
them to the innkeeper, and said, 'Take care of him;
and when I come back, I will repay you whatever more
you spend.' Which of these three, do you think, was
a neighbor to the man who fell into the hands of the
robbers?" He said, "The one who showed him mercy."
Jesus said to him, "Go and do likewise."*

—Luke 10:29-37

Let this sink in: The way that you love others is the way you love God. If you love others well, then you are loving God well. If you don't, well then . . . you aren't.

We are called to love our neighbor like we would love ourselves. We will explore "the who" and "the how" of carrying it out this week. Last week we explored and then engaged in devotional practices that deepen our relationship with God and keep us on the path of love. Regularly praying, reflecting on Scripture, and worshiping God fill our tanks for the journey. Yet, if we engage in all these acts of devotion, but don't love others—we've somehow missed the mark. To continue our quest to grow as love practitioners, we must dig more deeply into what loving our neighbor as ourselves actually means and looks like. The good news is that right there in Luke's Gospel, we have an important story that beautifully illustrates the answer.

The lawyer nails Jesus' question in verse 26 by referencing Deuteronomy 6:5 and Leviticus 19:18. Being well-versed and well-trained, it's probable that this man knew the ins and outs of Hebrew law. Leviticus 19:18 states, "You shall not take vengeance or bear a grudge against any of your people, but you shall love your neighbor as yourself: I am the LORD." To him, "neighbor" was most likely any member of the Hebrew nation, and maybe even extending to a resident alien. The lawyer and any others present would have understood that enacting revenge or holding grudges toward neighbors was not the way of love. In the Hebrew, the word for neighbor is *rea* (rā'·ah).* In the Greek language the word is *plesion* (plā-sē'-on).† Both words mean one who is near, fellow citizen, or friend.

The astute answer of the lawyer led Jesus to affirm that if one were to live out loving God with all his or her heart, soul, strength, and mind, *and* love one's neighbor as oneself—this person would indeed live, inheriting eternal life. The lawyer could have left it right there, but like many lawyers, he couldn't resist. He wanted to know, "Who is my neighbor?" The boldness of Jesus' claim that eternal life is connected to the Greatest Commandment should make us want to know the answer to that question, too. Before we continue with the remainder of Luke's story, let's state the obvious: *People long to love and be loved.* Love is the thing that knits us together. This is true whether people believe in God or not. Christians believe that the longing originates from God, infused into our being. I suspect if we were to conduct a survey asking about the key to living a life of meaning and purpose, somehow it would tie back to love and close relationships. Family, spouses, kids, friends, and other significant relationships would be lifted up as paramount to life. And that is beautiful, right, and good. Christians are called to protect, support, and nurture the people closest to us. Loving those closest to us isn't just a Christian thing, it's a human thing. So here's the rub: if everyone—Christians, secular humanists, "spiritual, not religious" folks, Jews, Muslims, Buddhists, atheists, agnostics, and Hindus—has a deeply ingrained desire to love, which manifests itself by nurturing the people and relationships close to us, then what differentiates followers of Jesus?

---

* "H7453—rea'—Strong's Hebrew Lexicon (KJV)," Blue Letter Bible, https://www .blueletterbible.org//lang/lexicon/lexicon.cfm?Strongs=H7453&t=KJV, accessed November 28, 2018.

† "G4139—plēsion—Strong's Greek Lexicon (KJV)," Blue Letter Bible, https://www .blueletterbible.org//lang/lexicon/lexicon.cfm?Strongs=G4139&t=KJV, Accessed November 28, 2018.

The Jewish people who heard the exchange between Jesus and the lawyer knew they were to love other Jews. Leviticus states that love was for "any of your people," and Jews were not to hold grudges or take vengeance on those closest to them. But they believed that loving people outside of that circle wasn't what the Greatest Commandment required.

Christians, however, know that Jesus radically broadened the definition of neighbor, illustrating that loving your neighbor means loving people outside the circle. Yet somehow when we look around at our lives, communities, and churches, we mostly see people just like us. The old saying that "the most segregated hour of the week is on Sunday morning" is true for a reason. Human beings have a propensity to be drawn to people similar to themselves; it is where we are most comfortable. We cluster with people who look like us, think like us, believe like us, act like us, and vote like us.

To only love those closest to us is to miss the depth and vastness of the Greatest Commandment. That doesn't mean we aren't to love those closest to us. Even though loving our messy families can be a formidable challenge in and of itself, it is the most natural and easiest kind of love. So, of course, love your family, friends, church, tribe, and your actual neighbors that live around you. Do it and do it extravagantly.

But to follow in the way of Jesus will mean we must extend our love outside our well-known and well-traveled circles.

The Scandal of the Good Samaritan

I am sure that everyone listening was eagerly anticipating Jesus' response to the lawyer's question so that it could be critiqued, compared, and debated. Jesus' response was clear, challenging, and downright shocking. Rather than using legalese, he masterfully narrated a dramatic story that vividly embodied what being a neighbor meant. It had an unlikely hero and unlikely fools. And it draws the circle bigger. Many Christians are familiar with the parable of the good

Samaritan. But the scandalous nature of the story escapes us today. It doesn't punch like it would in the first century. When you hear the word *Samaritan*, what are the words that come to your mind? I suspect they would be adjectives to describe a person who was kind, generous, merciful, or helpful.

I can assure you that whatever words that came to you would *not* have been the ones that crossed the lips of any Hebrew when they described a Samaritan in the first century. The Samaritans and Jews despised each other because each group thought they had the true religion. Samaritans were originally from the Northern Kingdom and part Jewish, but were considered by Jews to be mixed race. One principle argument between them was the location of the true place to worship. Jews believed it was Mount Zion in Jerusalem, and Samaritans believed it was Mount Gerizim. Jews were convinced that Samaritans held erroneous beliefs and practices and lacked purity. For those familiar with Harry Potter, the way Jews saw Samaritans would be akin to the way Slytherin pure-blood witches and wizards viewed half-bloods and Muggles. They were hated, looked-down-upon, second-class people. Having a Samaritan as the hero of Jesus' story would have been absolutely shocking and, frankly, insulting to a Jew.

One way for us to truly understand the way the story was heard when Jesus told it is to insert a group or a person for whom we have much disdain into the Samaritan's role in the story. Make sure that it's a person or a group that has different values, has enacted wrongs, or are folks we don't think deserve help. It could be a person who is liberal, conservative, a politician, your boss, your ex-spouse, a Ku Klux Klan member, someone from the new atheist movement, the Islamic State of Iraq and Syria (ISIS), the Taliban, whomever. Imagine Jesus using the name or member from the group you disdain as the one who acts as the neighbor. And then after that, place yourself or people from your group or church as the Levite and priest. That might begin to approach the shock of Jesus' answer.

In his story, Jesus describes a man heading from Jerusalem to Jericho. Those listening probably would have been familiar with the dicey and dangerous trail connecting the two cities. Beaten, stripped, and left for dead, the wounded man is seen first by the priest who "passed on the other side." That's an important phrase. Next up, the Levite. Surely he will be the man who comes to the rescue, right? Nope. He too "passes on the other side." These two should have been the heroes of the story, but they aren't. They are religious and know the law, but don't get involved. Now comes a dreaded Samaritan (or insert any group that you dislike). He engaged with the severely wounded man lying helplessly in the road. He was moved to action. He invested his time, attention, and money. He went the extra mile to ensure that the beaten man was cared for.

After telling the story, Jesus again asks the lawyer another question. "Which of these three, do you think, was a neighbor to the man who fell into the hands of the robbers?" (Luke 10:36). The lawyer nails the answer like he did to the question of how to inherit eternal life, but chooses not to utter the word *Samaritan* here. He said, "The one who showed him mercy." An unlikely hero who shows all of us who our neighbor is and how we are to love. Scandalous.

Won't You Be My Neighbor?

Recently, people have been enthralled with the 2018 documentary film *Won't You Be My Neighbor?*, which catalogs the life and legacy of Fred Rogers. For thirty-one years, the Presbyterian minister educated children and infused them with messages of love and safety through the popular children's television program *Mister Rogers' Neighborhood* on PBS. From what I've observed, Fred Rogers has become somewhat of a modern-day prophet with a soft voice, a kind heart, and a penetrating message. The film was filled with inspiring and powerful moments, but few were more powerful than when Fred Rogers made the decision to invite Francois Clemmons to join the cast as a police officer in 1968.

He was the first African American to have a recurring role on a kids' TV series. In an interview, Francois described it like this, "Fred came to me and said, 'I have this idea: You could be a police officer.'... I grew up in the ghetto. I did not have a positive opinion of police officers. [They] were siccing police dogs and water hoses on people."[*]

Then in 1969, at the height of segregation, Rogers lived out the message of Jesus. In that time, public fountains, public transportation, restaurants, public schools, and (most notably for this point) the public pools had become closed circles of segregation. Under Jim Crow laws, blacks and whites couldn't swim together, and many pools were for whites only; this was fueled by a fear that African Americans carried disease. Episode 1065 opened in the typical manner, except that Mister Rogers didn't put on the well-known cardigan, but instead opened the show in the front yard with an encounter with Officer Clemmons. On the front yard set was a kiddie pool filled with water. Rogers invited Officer Clemmons to take a break from his work and join him to cool his feet. Together, brown and white feet rested in the pool for all to see.

If that wasn't scandalous enough, it went a bit further. As Officer Clemmons was getting out of the pool, Mister Rogers helped him dry his feet.[†] In a time filled with fear, racism, and hate, Rogers gave a visual of loving your neighbor as yourself.

Seeing Jesus in Strange Places

There is a park bench prominently placed on our church's downtown campus on a main road. On it there is a man who sleeps twenty-four hours a day. The presumably homeless man's face and

---

[*] NPR Staff, "Walking the Beat in Mr. Rogers' Neighborhood, Where a New Day Began Together," NPR, March 11, 2016, https://www.npr.org/2016/03/11/469846519/walking-the-beat-in-mr-rogers-neighborhood-where-a-new-day-began-together.

[†] Hannah Anderson, "Won't You Be My Neighbor? Reconciliation and Foot-Washing in *Mister Rogers' Neighborhood*," *Christ and Pop Culture*, March 24, 2016, https://christandpopculture.com/wont-you-be-my-neighbor-mister-rogers/.

hands are obscured, well hidden under a blanket. But not his feet; they are poking out for all to see. Although it looks very real, it isn't a real person, but a sculpture conceptualized and created by artist Timothy Schmalz.[*]

On more than a few occasions, I have witnessed people being startled by it, thinking a person was sleeping on the bench. Others walk curiously by, peering at it from afar. Once a person discovers that it's not a human but a sculpture, they will sometimes draw near for a closer look. And that's when the revelation comes! On the feet are nail wounds, revealing that it is Jesus who sleeps, hidden in plain sight. Sometimes it can be an uncomfortable revelation. The provocative piece of art is meant to challenge and pull its viewers into discomfort.

The piece is titled *Homeless Jesus*, visually depicting Matthew 25.[†] The first identical work was installed in Toronto in 2013, and the artist will only allow one per city. As followers of Christ, we must see God in places where we'd rather not, in the places and people we'd rather avoid, and even in the shadows of our own lives.

Two important questions come to mind: Who are the people whom you would rather pass on the other side of the road? Who is suffering in your community that everyone seems to be ignoring?

After the lawyer says that people who show mercy are the lovers of neighbors, Jesus says, "Go and do likewise."

Like *Homeless Jesus*, the good Samaritan offers a similar revelation— showing that loving our neighbor includes people on the margins, people who are suffering, and people who need help to survive. To do that will mean venturing toward places we'd prefer not or that are foreign or strange and reaching out to people we don't understand. I don't know where or to whom God is inviting you to go, but I suspect

---

[*] John Burnett, "Statue of a Homeless Jesus Startles a Wealthy Community," NPR, April 13, 2014, https://www.npr.org/2014/04/13/302019921/statue-of-a-homeless-jesus-startles-a -wealthy-community.

[†] Timothy P. Schmalz, *Homeless Jesus*, 2013, bronze sculpture, 36 x 84 x 24", Toronto and various cities, Sculpture by Timothy P. Schmalz, https://www.sculpturebytps.com/large -bronze-statues-and-sculptures/homeless-jesus/, accessed August 28, 2018.

it will involve taking steps out from your circle and will pull you out of your comfort zone. But as you do, you will be living the Greatest Commandment and growing as a love practitioner.

The Samaritan Security Guard

Remember the way that the Levite and priest passed to the other side of the road to avoid the beaten man? They saw the mess just like the Samaritan, but they chose not to go near. Instead, they went the other way. They didn't want to get involved. Maybe they were scared. Maybe they thought that the wounded man somehow brought it on himself. Perhaps they had sympathy, but they didn't act. We will never know. But by avoiding him, they were able to quell any compassion for their fellow man.

And often, sadly, that is the normal, worldly response to suffering. We think the situation is too complex, or we don't have time, money, or training to deal with issues or people in trouble. Or we fear that we'd be enabling the person or are sure that somebody else will surely handle it. As followers of Jesus, loving our neighbor means that we must see the brokenness and suffering of all people with a different vision. Not as people or places to avoid, but as ones to go near. It says that the Samaritan *saw* the man and his circumstances, *drew near*, and was *moved with pity*. This verb "draw near" is important and used in Luke when Jesus sees suffering. It is used when he healed a hemorrhaging woman and when he fed the crowd by multiplying the food. It's the same verb that Luke used when Jesus healed a demon-possessed man. Over and over again, drawing near was the crucial first step toward loving a neighbor and venturing outside of the circle.

When I was in college, I was a mess. I was active in my addiction, causing problems and wreckage just about wherever I went. In my sophomore year, I was living in an apartment complex, and we had large, frequent, and loud parties. On one particularly loud and boisterous evening, I got into a verbal and near-physical altercation with one of the security guards. I didn't remember it, but I was told about it the next day. Let's just say, it wasn't good. And as you could imagine, I wasn't the most popular resident with the security staff.

But one of the security guards—a giant of a man—was very kind to me after the incident. For some reason, he saw me in a different way. He treated me with kindness and befriended me. I couldn't understand why he didn't avoid me like the other security guards did. He introduced me to his wife, brought me a birthday present, and did a bunch of other acts of kindness. Eventually he brought me a Bible (which I politely declined) and invited me to his church (which I also declined). And even though my receptivity to religion and Jesus was close to an all-time low, he planted a seed. He reintroduced me to faith in a way in which I had never experienced. He was very different from me and from the other pushy Christians I had encountered. I don't even remember this guy's name. He moved away soon after that year, but continued to write to me every month or two for about six months. I imagine I'm a distant memory. Even though I never responded to his invitations, his kindness made a profound impact on me. He will never know how significant this effect was on my life.

The security guard was the Samaritan. I was the beaten man lying in the road—I just didn't know it. He saw through differences, my rugged exterior, and macho behavior. He sensed my woundedness. He could have just moved on. But he went outside his circle and pushed through any apprehension he might have had. Like the good Samaritan, he saw a wounded man, was filled with compassion, and drew near. He did what he could to bind up my wounds. He loved his neighbor.

In what ways can you be the security guard to others? To whom are you called? It's yours to discover. We can better imitate the good Samaritan and the security guard as we:

1. see those who suffer,
2. experience compassion for those outside our circle,
3. draw near to those in need, and
4. act.

Many of you have been imitating the good Samaritan in your faith walk already. You are venturing outside your comfort zone and circles. You know the places and the people to whom you are called. And for those who believe that they have yet to make a beginning, it is possible you have already made progress without knowing it.

We'll explore those four ways to imitate the good Samaritan soon because loving our neighbor takes discernment. While not everyone is called to every issue, each of us is called to people outside our circles. It may only be for a season, or it could be a lifelong direction. But God prompts and uses disciples of Jesus to go into places and minister to people throughout neighborhoods, communities, cities, and the world. And by doing so, the love of Jesus Christ is made tangible.

Look and Listen for People on the Road

A first good opportunity to love a neighbor outside your circle as yourself is to take note of the suffering around us. Sometimes it will be right in front of us, but other times we will have to search for it. I want to be clear that you don't need to engage every need or issue. Nor do you need to help every person, but you can *see* people and even speak their names. Every person, even those most blinded from themselves and God, bears the divine mark of God.

I mentioned that you have made a start already to be the good Samaritan even if you don't know it. The Spirit of God is already at work in you. Reflect on these questions; write down your answers. It just might be that the answers hold clues as to how you can more deliberately love your neighbor.

- Where do you look at the world and your heart breaks?
- Where do you look at your local community and feel anger?
- Where does your heart feel compassion for those on the margins?

A place in the world where my heart breaks is people experiencing homelessness. I have felt drawn and called to single men who, because of their background (felonies, addiction, evictions), have a hard time getting and retaining housing. Even so, I usually don't give out money to people on the roadside while I'm stopped at intersections. One afternoon, however, I was on the toll road heading home, taking my normal route, and as I was driving, I had a strong sense that I needed to pull off on the next exit. Surprisingly, I actually heeded the prompting. As I headed down the ramp, I noticed a man standing at the intersection with a sign. The light was red, and I was the only car stopped. From his appearance, he looked like life had beaten him down. I sometimes have food or water in my car, but on this day I had none. No cash, no change, nothing to give. I felt a bit of angst because I thought the prompting to pull off might have meant that I was to give this man something tangible. I rolled down the window and said, "Hey, my name is Justin. I am so sorry; I don't have anything to give you, but thought I'd ask you your name and see if there are specific ways I can pray for you." He said his name, and I said hello. He slowly made his way to my window. He bent down so he could better see me. He had bright, penetrating eyes, the kind of eyes that pierce your soul. He looked intently at me and responded, "You gave me a better gift than money or food. Thank you for saying my name, Justin. Thank you." As I pulled away, I wept. I wept because I recognized for the first time in a long time the risen Christ. He was hidden in plain sight. Sometimes people just need to hear their name or to be seen.

As Yourself

Forming our answers to the posed questions about where our hearts break, what we are angered by, and where we look upon the world and where our heart experiences compassion will assist in the discovery of where God might be prompting us to draw near. Praying and asking God to reveal the issues or people to which we are called can also pave the way forward.

But there's more.

Luke reminds us that the commandment is not just to "love your neighbor," but to "love your neighbor *as yourself*." Those are two peculiar, cryptic, but critical words. What does it mean to love another person "as yourself"?

Well, we might conclude that it is a command to love ourselves as part of the process of loving others. That would be helpful advice, especially if any of us were dealing with old wounds from our past. Those wounds would make it hard to love ourselves, diminishing our ability to love others as a result.

I have a friend whom I have known for a long time and love very much who isn't very proficient at loving himself or his neighbor. In fact, he's terrible at it. His inability to love himself stems from many wounds dealt to him growing up as a gay person in a very strict "religious" home filled with instability, violence, and drunken behavior. You know the kind. Because of this, he walks around in a shroud of guilt, shame, and self-loathing. Lack of trust and an inability to believe in a benevolent God have handicapped his being, resulting in patterns of destructive thoughts, addictive behaviors, and good old-fashioned self-sabotage. He wears anger, self-pity, and negativity openly, but these barely cover the hurt right under the surface. Needless to say, loving his neighbor as himself is difficult. He sometimes treats others like he treats himself—harshly.

When we don't (or are unable to) love ourselves, our ability to love those around us—whether they are inside or outside our circle—is greatly diminished. Maybe that's what Luke means in telling us to love your neighbor as yourself. When we don't (or can't) love ourselves, we are affected like a virus infects computer software. If you want to love your neighbor as yourself, begin by healing any wounds infecting your ability to love.

There's another possibility. The Greek word for "as" can also be translated "as if it is." Think about the possible implication of that translation. Love your neighbor *as if it were your own self*. As if that person were connected to you, interdependent with you, coequal with you. In other words, as much as we might fixate on all the ways we are different from one another, maybe the parable of the good Samaritan would want us to remember that we are all essentially the same children of the same God, redeemed by the same Christ. We may look different, act differently, or be more or less wounded, but we all are to be loved.

God's love is unconditional (*agape*), without expectation or demand for return. God does not love us so that we might love God back. That is how we often love, with a conditional, transactional expectation that we would get something in return. And that is not how we are to love our neighbor, either.

Instead, God loves us so that in and through that love, we might be transformed into more loving beings—love practitioners. God loves us so that our capacity to love can increase, and therefore love ourselves and others in greater ways. That is the way we are to love our neighbor: not to get something in return, but to increase their capacity to love, just as God as increased ours. Sometimes it means carrying some of their burden and wounds, and sometimes others carry ours. It is to "love it forward," so that God can transform the world, one loving relationship at a time. And in the process, we become more like Christ.

Now, a section on loving our neighbor should include some practical, biblical steps to do it. How does the New Testament speak of loving others into community with one another? One way is through spiritual gifts. These are capacities given to us by the Holy Spirit for the purpose of fulfilling the mission of making disciples of Jesus Christ who participate in God's transformation of the world. They help us find our place to serve.

Service, Gifts, and Time

Every disciple of Jesus is a minister. There is something referred to as "the priesthood of all believers" or "the ministry of all Christians" that proclaims that all followers of Jesus are called, gifted, and to be sent out to love God and neighbor. While some people can get freaked out by that statement, Scripture illustrates its truth. It will mean that you have to sacrifice, but that's a part of traveling the narrow road. At times you will have to invest time that you feel like you don't have and money you'd prefer to spend elsewhere. And at times, you may be called to serve in areas or with people that stretch your level of comfort.

The good news is that God gives us spiritual gifts so that we can do it! Spiritual gifts are not natural talents, although they may be closely related. Gifts from the spirit are to be used to build the church. Just like grace, they are not something that we earn. God gives them freely. Romans 12:6-8, Ephesians 4:11-12, and 1 Corinthians 12:8-10 catalog the different spiritual gifts. And you have at least one, probably more.

There are a variety of spiritual gifts assessments that can help you with your discernment. In my experience, we usually have two or three, at most, primary gifts. We may have attributes of others, but generally there are a couple that, when employed, we are able to use to best live out our ministry of servanthood. Spiritual gifts are best discovered and confirmed in a community of faith. The church should help disciples discover their gifts and send these folks out to serve.

I was blown away when I first learned what my spiritual gifts could be at the concluding weekend retreat of a nine-month weekly Bible study. Group members were tasked with writing down the spiritual gifts that they thought other group members had. We then shared them with one another. Over and over again, two gifts kept being named by the group members for me. As I was a relatively new Christian, I was excited to learn more about God and the gifts God had given me. The next step was finding my role in the body of Christ, my way to serve.

Dietrich Bonhoeffer described the body of Christ metaphor like this: "The body is the form. So the church is not a religious community of those who revere Christ, but Christ who has taken form among human beings."* The "body of Christ" metaphor comes from Paul (Saul was his Jewish name). He says in Romans, "For as in one body we have many members, and not all the members have the same function, so we, who are many, are one body in Christ, and individually we are members one of another. We have gifts that differ according to the grace given to us" (Romans 12:4-6).

---

* Dietrich Bonhoeffer, *Dietrich Bonhoeffer Works, Volume 6: Ethics*, ed. Clifford J. Green, trans. Reinhard Krauss, Charles C. West, and Douglas W. Stott (Minneapolis: Fortress Press, 2005), 96, https://books.google.ca/books?id=XLqkvQB5oO4C&printsec=frontcover&hl =en#v=snippet&q=%22religious%20community%22&f=false, accessed November 19, 2018.

Prior to his conversion, Paul was a strict Jew and given the power to persecute people following Jesus. On the road to Damascus, he has a white light experience, is struck blind, and hears a voice say, "Why do you persecute me?" Scared and confused, he asks, "Who are you, Lord?" The voice responds, "I am Jesus, whom you are persecuting" (Acts 9:1-9, especially vv. 4, 5, 6). This would have been very puzzling to him, not just because he was blind, but because Jesus of Nazareth was executed long ago. While Paul thought he was eradicating a small sect of people, what he discovered was that they were Jesus' body, his flesh and blood in the world—and the body of Christ metaphor was constructed.

The body of Christ is a collection of believers who live out Jesus' love. Some of you have been gifted to serve as Jesus' hands, his feet, his mouth, his ears, or heart. No matter, each is important if it is to work and function in unity. The church is God's very improbable redemption plan. We live it out as we grow in our love for God and neighbor, discover our spiritual gifts, and put them to use in the body of Christ.

What are your gifts? Have you found your role in the body of Christ?

Heart Filled with Compassion

We will end where we began. How we love others is how we love God. To love our neighbor means loving those closest to us, loving people outside our circle, and, yes, even loving ourselves. It will mean seeing the suffering around us with new eyes and with a heart filled with compassion. The compassion will compel us to draw near to those who are wounded rather than pass by them on the other side, and act in some way to relieve their suffering just as though we were caring for ourselves. And while our call and service will take different shapes, discovering and employing our spiritual gifts will help us find our role in the body of Christ.

And all of it matters to God and the world. Intentionally loving our neighbor is not only an honor and privilege, it is participating in God's redemption of the world here and now, as we wait for the one to come. And as we follow the pattern of the good Samaritan and the security guard, love will flourish.

But there is one last aspect of living out the Greatest Command-ment that is the hardest of all. We held that off for the last week: loving our enemy.

Week 2
DEVOTIONALS

Day 8: Loving Those Closest

Scripture

The commandment we have from him is this: those who love God must love their brothers and sisters also.
—1 John 4:21

Loving our neighbor as ourselves includes those closest to us—spouses, significant others, children, family, friends, and our faith community. These are the people who should be the easiest to love and whom we can sometimes take for granted.

My grandmother Eva was the matriarch of my faith. Until age nine, I spent most every Friday, Saturday, and Sunday at her and my grandfather's house. They took me to church and were instrumental in shaping me into the man I am today. When I moved thirty minutes away to Florida, our visits were frequent. But when I hit a demanding season of life with my beginning a young family and starting a new campus for the church, our time spent together dwindled. When my grandmother was in her early nineties, her health had begun to wane, and it was a bad fall that had her confined to her apartment that snapped me out of my complacency. The last couple years of her life, I began visiting weekly again. It was a rich time where we talked about the past, the present, and the future. She shared about her march toward death, her faith, unfulfilled dreams, and the things for which she was grateful. By the grace of God, I got to feel like nothing was left unsaid when she passed away.

On this day, remember to love those nearest to you. It could be a call to tell someone how much you love them, an encouraging word to your spouse or child, a simple hug, or an act of service. Perhaps you could reach out to someone who has helped you love God or shaped your faith to tell him or her how much you appreciate them.

In your prayer time today, reflect on how you might love the neighbors nearest to you. Plan a few intentional acts of love toward those closest to you.

Reflection Questions

- Who are the people in your family you can love today?
- How can you express your love for your extended family today?
- How can you express your love for your brothers and sisters in Christ?

Prayer

God, thank you for those closest to me—family, friends, mentors, children, and other people you have placed in my life. Help me to love them with my full heart, with my words and actions. Amen.

Challenge

To show those closest to you how much you love them.

Day 9: See the Suffering

Scripture

Then the LORD said, "I have observed the misery of my people who are in Egypt; I have heard their cry on account of their taskmasters. Indeed, I know their sufferings, and I have come down to deliver them from the Egyptians, and to bring them up out of that land to a good and broad land, a land flowing with milk and honey.... The cry of the Israelites has now come to me; I have also seen how the Egyptians oppress them. So

*come, I will send you to Pharaoh to bring my people,
the Israelites, out of Egypt." But Moses said to God,
"Who am I that I should go to Pharaoh, and bring the
Israelites out of Egypt?"*

—*Exodus 3:7-11*

In Exodus, the Israelites are enslaved and oppressed for many years. God sees it and wants something to be done about it. He calls Moses. Understandably, Moses initially resists and provides multiple reasons why he wouldn't be suited to fulfill the monumental task.

I don't think Moses is unique in either the call he receives or the resistance he puts forth. God hasn't stopped seeing suffering or calling his followers to it. There is plenty of suffering in our communities and the world. We can't engage it all nor should we. But there is suffering and people to which God is inviting us to go. It may be that God is calling you to familiar places and people or to unfamiliar places and new people who are suffering. But often before we go, we must see it. Like the Samaritan who saw the beaten man, we too must see with God's eyes. That often will penetrate and break down the excuses we have created in our heads and hearts.

In this time today, practice *Lectio Divina* with Exodus 3:7-11.

Reflection Questions

- Refer to the question from the chapter: Where do you look at the world and your heart breaks?
- Who is suffering in your community whom everyone seems to be ignoring?
- What excuses do you make for not being sent?

Prayer

God, you see the suffering in my life, in the community, and the world. Inspire me to see the suffering to which I am called. Prompt me, make me aware of your still gentle voice, inviting me to be sent to whomever you choose. Help me to be courageous in the midst of any doubt or fear I have about engaging. Amen.

Challenge

To reflect upon and see the suffering in the world.

Day 10: Unbind

Scripture

Jesus began to weep....

Then Jesus, again greatly disturbed, came to the tomb. It was a cave, and a stone was lying against it. Jesus said, "Take away the stone." Martha, the sister of the dead man, said to him, "Lord, already there is a stench because he has been dead four days." Jesus said to her, "Did I not tell you that if you believed, you would see the glory of God?" So they took away the stone. And Jesus looked upward and said, "Father, I thank you for having heard me. I knew that you always hear me, but I have said this for the sake of the crowd standing here, so that they may believe that you sent me." When he had said this, he cried with a loud voice, "Lazarus, come out!" The dead man came out, his hands and feet bound with strips of cloth, and his face wrapped in a cloth. Jesus said to them, "Unbind him, and let him go."
—John 11:35, 38-44

Lazarus had been dead four days. Disappointment, confusion, and pain were consuming the sisters and the community. This wasn't the way it was supposed to be. The sisters had sent word to Jesus about his sickness and expected him to come quickly. They waited and hoped. He didn't arrive on time, and the sisters couldn't understand why. Jesus was deeply disturbed by the loss of his friend and their pain. He wept.

God is not unaffected by pain, suffering, questions about why, or loss. We believe in a God who is "with us" in and through the grief of life.

Jesus makes things that were once dead come alive. It is true for our lives now and later. In this story, Jesus shouts for Lazarus to come out of the tomb. He came out wrapped up in the death rags. Jesus raised him from the dead, but it was the community that Jesus commanded to set him free from the death rags. *Community unbinds us.* Whether it is death, addiction, tragedy, or our own sin, being in community helps set us free.

Reflection Questions

- Where are the places in our own lives that we need God to resuscitate us?
- Where are the places in our own lives that we need others to help unbind us?
- Where are places in the community or world that we can help unbind others?

Prayer

God, thank you for bringing things that are dead to life. Show me the ways I can unbind others and allow others to unbind me. In Jesus' name I pray. Amen.

Challenge

To let the community unbind you.

Day 11: Success Versus Significance

Scripture 1:

> So teach us to count our days
> that we may gain a wise heart.
>
> —*Psalm 90:12*

Scripture 2:

> *Search me, O God, and know my heart;*
> *test me and know my thoughts.*
>
> —*Psalm 139:23*

I met Joe after he began dating a friend and member of our congregation. He was raised in the church, but had not been rooted in a congregation or engaged in cultivating his relationship with God for a while. He was in the middle of life, had recently gone through a divorce, and was very successful in business. Feeling unfulfilled and discontented with his current career, he sensed that he was being called to something new. He just didn't know what. As Stephen R. Covey said in his bestseller *The 7 Habits of Highly Effective People*, It's incredibly easy…to work harder and harder at climbing the ladder of success only to discover it's leaning against the wrong wall."*

Joe's faith began to flourish; he engaged in worship and a men's group and wanted to find a way to make a difference. He was invited to read Bob Buford's book *Halftime*, which is about the transition from the first half of life to the second.† What he learned was that he was being called to live a life more dedicated to Jesus Christ—to focus on a life of significance rather than a life of success. He wanted to place his ladder on a different wall.

Joe began exploring ways that his job could be a vocation. He started a new business that provides houses for low-income people, many of whom have histories that would prevent them from attaining housing. His circle got bigger. He sat with people he had never before been in contact with and learned about their situations. Joe shared *his* halftime story and offered them an opportunity to step forward into their second half.

Joe included "second half" in his company name so that he would be reminded of his call and why he was doing it. In his witness, he

---

* Stephen R. Covey, *The 7 Habits of Highly Effective People* (New York: Simon & Schuster, 2004), 98.

† See Bob Buford, *Halftime: Changing Your Game Plan from Success to Significance* (Grand Rapids, MI: Zondervan, 1994).

shares not only how God has shifted his life, but the way that it has shifted the lives of his tenants.

But that wasn't all. God continued to work on his heart.

He discovered his spiritual giftedness and passion. He invests financially in the mission of the church and serves people in need. He was sparked to donate the use of one of his houses to a ministry that provides dignified, safe, and affordable housing to single men experiencing homelessness. And he provides the oversight and guidance to the ministry, sharing his property management expertise. Joe looked around and discovered that God was calling him to a new thing. God ignited his desire to love his neighbor. Through Joe's awareness and willingness, God is making a way through the wilderness for neighbors who are struggling.

Joe has pivoted from a life of success to a life of significance. He did it through engaging in a relationship with God and the church, discovering his giftedness and passion, and investing his time, his talent as a business owner, and his money.

In your community or in your church, there is a gap. And it is in the shape of you. Only you can fill it. And by so doing, your ladder will be placed on a different wall.

Today, practice *Lectio Divina* with today's Scripture or with 1 Corinthians 12:4-11, 14-20.

Write your obituary. Reflect on the fact that your days are numbered. Write out how you would like your obituary to read. Include the way God has used and will use you in your family, church, and community. Make it aspirational, including the things you have done, who you are, and who you are called to be.

Reflection Questions

- Where is your ladder positioned?
- What opportunities could you explore in your congregation or in the community that fill a need? If you could solve any issue faced by your community what would it be?
- What does living a life of significance mean to you?

Prayer

God, I give thanks for the ways you have loved me and gifted me to love others. Search my heart, show me my spiritual gifts and how to invest my time, talent, and resources. Lead me to more deeply serve my neighbor. Amen.

Challenge

To think about your legacy and make steps toward living a life of significance if you aren't already.

Day 12: A Bigger Circle

Scripture

> *For once you were darkness, but now in the Lord you are light. Live as children of light—for the fruit of the light is found in all that is good and right and true. Try to find out what is pleasing to the Lord. Take no part in the unfruitful works of darkness, but instead expose them. For it is shameful even to mention what such people do secretly; but everything exposed by the light becomes visible, for everything that becomes visible is light. Therefore it says,*
>
>   *"Sleeper, awake!*
>   *Rise from the dead,*
>   *and Christ will shine on you."*
>
> —*Ephesians 5:8-14*

It was an unexpected connection. We had eaten in silence together on a number of occasions but never spoke. But during my second-to-last day at the monastery, I noticed his shirt, which suggested that he was part of a twelve-step fellowship. I whispered to him about it, and he confirmed. I indicated that I was too, so we went to an area where we could talk freely. We hit it off, having conversation and sharing stories like we were old friends. We conversed about the way silent prayer and meditation had bolstered our journeys. We decided to meet later in the Guadalupe Chapel, which was in the basement, to meditate together and continue our rich conversation. The chapel was dark and secluded, a space less utilized by monastery guests. We talked for hours and no topic seemed to be off limits: our families, upbringings, wreckage from the past, and the new life that God had given us.

But then it got *really real*. In the dark recesses of that chapel, he confessed something that he had never shared with anyone: he was extremely racist. And it was eating him up. He had begun to work with an African American man in his twelve-step program, and their relationship was drawing him to question his previously held attitudes and perspectives. He knew that it was wrong, but a lifetime of imbedded hate and feeling superior was making it hard for him to let go.

He knew in his heart that God was calling him to draw a bigger circle. We prayed together that God would penetrate his unwillingness to open his heart and his mind and enable him to walk in the way that leads to life.

That day, in that holy place, he exposed his darkness to light. When we allow our darkness to be exposed to light, it becomes visible. When it becomes visible, it becomes light. God's powerful love reveals to us the old ideas, biases, and perspectives that we must shed in order for us to love our neighbor more deeply. Go and do likewise.

Reflection Questions

- Do you have attitudes toward groups or a person that are hindering your ability to love?
- What are you hiding from the world?

Prayer

God, reveal to me the ideas or biases that prevent me from greater love of you and my neighbor. Instill in me a willingness to grow, to stretch, and allow your Light to transform my darkness. Amen.

Challenge

To let go of previously held ideas that keep you away from greater love.

Day 13: A Peach Cake

Scripture

> *He sat down opposite the treasury, and watched the crowd putting money into the treasury. Many rich people put in large sums. A poor widow came and put in two small copper coins, which are worth a penny. Then he called his disciples and said to them, "Truly I tell you, this poor widow has put in more than all those who are contributing to the treasury. For all of them have contributed out of their abundance; but she out of her poverty has put in everything she had, all she had to live on."*
>
> —*Mark 12:41-44*

I arrived at the park in downtown Tampa at 5 a.m. on the day before Easter. Our inaugural sunrise Easter service was the next day, and I wanted to see exactly where the sun would emerge (yes, I knew it would rise in the east), and pray over the space. As I walked around the park, I noticed this woman, her wheelchair, and her little dog were under the bandshell just starting to stir after a night's sleep. Later, I introduced myself and we began talking. She had moved to Tampa from San Diego after living on the street for twenty-five years. Her little dog, Professor, was her constant companion. It was a chance decision that had brought her to Tampa. I told her what I was doing and invited her to the Easter sunrise service. Later in the conversation, I discovered that she had been working with the police department's homeless liaison, and that in two weeks she was going to be placed in the fixed-income housing directly across the street from our congregation. She came to the sunrise service, and we kept in touch over the next week as she prepared to move in.

A week after she was housed, I invited Ruby to our monthly potluck. When she asked me what she could bring, I was tempted to tell her not to bring anything—she had just moved in. But I resisted. I told her to bring whatever she wanted and that we were grateful that she was part of our congregation.

That Sunday, I remember Ruby wheeling her wheelchair with Professor on it toward the church. I noticed that she was holding something: a peach cake made with the ingredients that she had had in her apartment. She wore a big smile and felt good about her participation.

I am so grateful to God that I didn't tell her not to worry about bringing something, as it would have denied her the opportunity to contribute. Something important would not have happened. Ruby gave what she had, and she was blessed by her participation, as was the whole community.

Like the widow, Ruby put in more than anyone else on that day.

Reflection Questions

- How are you investing your time and resources?
- Is there a place where you are being called to sacrifice?
- Who could you get to know who isn't in your normal circle?

Prayer

God, make me aware of my surroundings today and the way that I give to the world. Open my heart to give more fully to all those around me today. Amen.

Challenge

To see the way you give to the world.

Day 14: Rest

Scripture

> *Six days you shall work, but on the seventh day you*
> *shall rest; even in plowing time and in harvest time*
> *you shall rest.*
>
> —*Exodus 34:21*

Reflect on the past week. You have thought about how to best love those closest, the suffering that you see throughout the community, and how community can unbind. On days eleven, twelve, and thirteen, you reflected on what it would mean to live a life of significance rather than success, explored any attitudes or perspectives you are hiding in the dark, and pondered the place from which you give.

I hope you have remained faithful to the spiritual practices for two weeks. Praying, reading and reflecting on Scripture; remembering your blessings; and talking to God are deepening your relationship with God.

Today is a time to rest and remember that God is with you. Find a place to be quiet so you can reflect on the past week and reflect on the following questions.

Practice *Lectio Divina* with Luke 10:30-35 and take the word God gives you, saying it throughout your day.

Reflection Questions

- Where have you seen evidence of God at work in your life?
- How has God been speaking to you throughout the week?

Prayer

God, search my thoughts and heart. Help me to rest in you, to remember how much you love me. Today, give me a heart of worship and connect me to the gift of my life. Amen.

Challenge

**To rest on the sabbath and worship
with your faith community.**

Week 3
LOVING YOUR ENEMY

Week 3

LOVING YOUR ENEMY

"But I say to you that listen, Love your enemies, do good to those who hate you, bless those who curse you, pray for those who abuse you. If anyone strikes you on the cheek, offer the other also; and from anyone who takes away your coat do not withhold even your shirt. Give to everyone who begs from you; and if anyone takes away your goods, do not ask for them again. Do to others as you would have them do to you.

"If you love those who love you, what credit is that to you? For even sinners love those who love them. If you do good to those who do good to you, what credit is that to you? For even sinners do the same. If you lend to those from whom you hope to receive, what credit is that to you? Even sinners lend to sinners, to receive as much again. But love your enemies, do good, and lend, expecting nothing in return. Your reward will be great, and you will be children of the Most High; for he

is kind to the ungrateful and the wicked. Be merciful,
just as your Father is merciful.

—Luke 6:27-36

Who among you wants to do good to those who hate us? No one. Loving our family, friends, and those who are kind to us and love us comes with less effort. But Jesus' convicting words are "if you love those who love you, what credit is that to you? For even sinners love those who love them." Ouch. Is there any other teaching that feels more foreign to our sensibilities or unnatural to our human experience? Probably not. This teaching of Jesus in the Gospels to love one's enemies requires the most intentionality, willingness, and suspension of our egos. Calling it a challenge to love our enemies is understated.

So how can we do it?

The natural response that we have toward people who hurt, persecute, or abuse us is not to turn the other cheek, but to take an eye for an eye. Intuitively, we know that "righteous anger," while normal, weighs us down. Eventually, it blocks us off from relationship with Jesus Christ. Hate and hurt can turn into a heavy load to bear.

Not many people knew the negative impact of heavy loads better than Samuel Plimsoll, an advocate against a powerful shipping lobby in the nineteenth century. In his twenties, a failed endeavor left him poor and struggling. After he was able to get out of poverty, he never forgot the plight of those on the margins, and many believe that his own experience being poor shaped his advocacy for underpaid seamen who couldn't advocate for themselves. During that time, unprincipled owners overloaded their vessels with heavy cargo, making voyages likely to fail. These jam-packed ships came to be known as "coffin ships" because they would most always sink, losing both the cargo and the crew.* It was an industry practice to heavily insure the ships so owners would not lose out. Some ships were worth more at the bottom of the ocean than afloat.

---

* Simon Garfield, "The Bottom Line About Mr. Plimsoll," *The Guardian*, June 24, 2006, https://www.theguardian.com/books/2006/jun/25/biography.features.

Samuel Plimsoll made it his life's work to change this practice legislatively to protect the workers. The Plimsoll line—a reference point on a ship's hull that indicates the maximum depth the vessel may be safely immersed when loaded with cargo—is well known throughout boating and shipping.* A simple reference mark revolutionized the industry, helping save lives by ending the practice of coffin ships.

When we refuse to forgive and love our enemies, spiritually, we begin the process of building our own coffin ship. Before long, our ship will take on water.

Every one of us at one time or another has had the experience of hating someone or being wronged. If you haven't, you will. The wounds can be deep or slight, long lasting or short-lived, fresh or long-scarred. Even if somehow we contributed to the problem, praying for or loving our enemies doesn't come naturally. Lashing out in both overt and covert ways, feeling morally superior, and holding people in judgment flow more naturally than letting go.

I have good news and bad news. First, the good news: you are not alone. The mind is attracted to drama and hurt like flies are attracted to smelly dung. The way of the world and our instinctual desires would have us conspire, plan, and punish people for their misdeeds. I am not saying that there should not be outcomes for bad behavior, that there should not be boundaries, or that we should be naive doormats who mindlessly return to people who hurt us over and over again. What I am saying, and what I think the Scripture says clearly, is that when we are unwilling to forgive our enemies, we block ourselves off from being forgiven. When the heart gets locked up, the ability to love gets weakened. That's because the power of hate builds walls, walls create a prison that we will inhabit, and the prison cuts us off from relationship with God and neighbor.

If the good news is that it is normal, then here's the bad news: if you are to be a Jesus-follower, you must stop the cycle. You must

---

* National Oceanic and Atmospheric Administration, "What Is a Plimsoll Line?," National Ocean Service, last updated June 25, 2018, https://oceanservice.noaa.gov/facts/plimsoll-line .html.

not only pray for your enemies, but you must forgive them, too. And when possible, reconcile with them. Terrible, I know. It is the part of following Jesus that most ignore or would prefer to forget. Remember, no one said following Jesus would be easy. And if they did, they were lying or haven't done the difficult work of loving their enemies.

But we can find a way—with God's help. It will be an imperfect, possibly messy, and unsatisfying process. It may feel like we move three steps forward and then take a couple backward. No matter, our willingness to engage and take action will deepen and expand our knowledge of God. It will honor God and open us to a deeper sense of God's grace. It has the capacity to unburden us from people, places, and things that continue to weigh us down. We can be free.

But first, we must leave the comfort of the upper decks and descend to inspect the freight that is stored below.

Heavy Cargo in the Hold

There is cargo in the bowels of our spiritual ship. In boating vernacular, that's the section of the ship that is called a "hold." It is below the upper deck. If we are going to travel the narrow road of praying for and loving our enemies, we have to explore what we have packed away in our holds. The cargo may have been in there for a very long time or be very recent. Its weight comes from the anger, subtle superiorities, hatred, well-nurtured resentments, and long-forgotten grudges that we hold toward people.

So how, exactly, do we define our enemies? Good question. One possible definition is any person, group, institution, or tribe who has hurt us (directly or indirectly) or has hurt something or someone we care about. The damage could have happened to us individually, to loved ones, to friends, to the nation, or to the world. And because of the actions, beliefs, or values of that individual or group, we are angry. We may feel intense hatred toward them, or we may not. We may have planned or implemented elaborate schemes to get back at them and hold them accountable...or not. What is certain is that our enemies have negatively impacted our lives. They have affected our relationships, finances, the way we think about ourselves (self-concept), the way we feel about ourselves (self-worth), or what others think about us—not for the better.

The hurt that they caused (or are causing) and the animosity or apathy we have toward them weighs us down. And in many cases, we don't know how to forgive, pray for, or love them. And we don't want to.

Take a moment to picture a person's face who has hurt you or whom you would consider an enemy. Get an image of him or her in your mind's eye. It could have been from long ago or more recently. Now replay the circumstances that contributed to the way you feel. Think about their behavior, their words and malevolent intent, and the rejection, betrayal, abandonment or injury that resulted. How easily do the intense feelings return? Tapping into these memories and the feelings we were left with usually comes rather effortlessly. It is probable that we rarely—if ever—cross their minds, but they rent space in our heads for free. We brood and fantasize about the ways we wish we would have actually responded. We ruminate about imaginary conversations that we didn't have, but wish we did. We take pleasure in imagining that they receive the punishment that they deserve, or in contrast, that they would accept responsibility and recognize the error of their ways. These patterns often repeat over and over again, consciously or unconsciously, and hate begins to root in our hearts. For the Christian trying to love God and neighbor, it is disastrous. There is an old saying that "when you hold on to hate, it is like drinking poison in the hopes that your enemy will die." And you will die. Maybe not literally, but spiritually. Hatred grinds at our mental, emotional, and spiritual health; and the Scripture specifically instructs that we must recoil from it.

Inventory Your Cargo

The process of self-examination, confession, and forgiveness has been a part of the church since the beginning. What was once commonplace, however, has now faded into the background of contemporary Christianity. Alcoholics Anonymous and other twelve-step programs of recovery have embraced this practice and utilized it (much better than the current Church, in my opinion) to free many who suffer from the scourge of addiction. One of the steps of recovery has people make "a searching and fearless moral inventory" of themselves,* looking closely at the people who have wronged them, their own character flaws and fears, and their conduct. A powerful and often difficult part of the exercise is looking at the ways that the person contributed to creating the problem with their enemies. After completing the inventory, he or she confesses it to God, another trusted person, and themselves. What is revealed is their character, their wrongs, and the patterns that create cargo.†

Examining our motivations, character, and actions will help us to forgive.

> Some of you are thinking, "Yeah right. If you only knew what (insert name) has done, you couldn't forgive them either." You assert, "They have hurt me! They are unrepentant, and continue to go about life without any consequences. It is not fair." You may be correct that you can't currently forgive (name). And it is a normal protest.

But here's the kicker: *God*, who knew you before the formation of the world, who has chosen you and given you the Holy Spirit, *can*. All that is needed to begin is a mustard seed of willingness, or the willingness to pray to God about your unwillingness. A common misperception that stops people from embarking on the journey to forgive is the erroneous belief that biblical forgiveness means that you have to be in regular relationship with the person who wronged you. Forgiving your enemy doesn't always mean there is reconciliation,

---

* "The Twelve Steps of Alcoholics Anonymous," Alcoholics Anonymous World Services Inc., https://www.aa.org/assets/en_US/smf-121_en.pdf, accessed August 30, 2018.

† Bill W., *Alcoholics Anonymous*, third ed. (New York: Alcoholics Anonymous World Services Inc., 1976), 66, 72.

that suddenly everything is better, or that forgiving means you are holding hands and singing "Kumbaya." Reconciliation would be ideal, but there are situations and relationships that are toxic, where appropriate boundaries should be strictly maintained. Nevertheless, being a follower of Jesus means you are called to release any hatred and no longer hold ill will, offering them over to God's care so you that can release the power they have over you and move on. To forgive is to let go.

Postures Toward Forgiveness

While not exhaustive, there are a number of fairly common postures toward enemies and forgiveness. Perhaps you can find yourself in one of these (using the acronym **RUIN**):

Rejection—I have enemies but refuse to forgive them.
Unskilled—I have enemies, and I know I am supposed to forgive my enemies, but I don't know how.
Ignorance (or Lucky/Blind)—I have no enemies and no one to forgive.
Neglect (or Confused)—I forgive my enemies easily but reconcile too quickly or again and again.

The most common and understandable posture of the world is knowing that we have enemies but refuse to forgive them. We *reject* Jesus' call to forgive. Holding forgiveness from others emphasizes that we don't believe they deserve to be loved, prayed for, or forgiven for their misdeeds.

Jesus once told a story of why this doesn't work in the spiritual life.

In the parable, a king was settling the money he was owed with his slaves, and a slave with a large debt was brought to him. When the slave was unable to pay, it was ordered that all of his family and possession were to be sold so the payment could be settled. The slave begged the king to be patient and promised to pay him back. Out of compassion, the king not only released him, but he forgave the debt—

an extraordinary act of mercy. He freed him of all obligations. And that should have been the end of the story, but it wasn't. The same man who had just been shown this mercy came across another slave who owed him a much smaller sum. He grabbed him violently and demanded payment. The fellow slave pleaded in the same way and with the same words that the man demanding the payment did with the king. But the one who was shown mercy had none for the other. He had him thrown into prison. Word got back to king, and he was not pleased. He called the first man a wicked slave and asked "Should you not have had mercy on your fellow slave, as I had mercy on you?" And in anger the man was handed over until he could pay his entire debt. Jesus then warns, "So my heavenly Father will also do to every one of you, if you do not forgive your brother or sister from your heart" (see Matthew 18:23-35, especially vv. 33, 35).

For those of us who have experienced forgiveness in Christ and withhold forgiveness against our enemies, we become the slave in the story. We must pattern ourselves after Jesus; we must forgive because we have been forgiven—no matter how big of a task that is. If you are unwilling, then connect to the ways you have been forgiven. To begin, it is as simple as asking God to open your heart to be willing to forgive.

The second posture toward enemies is close to the first, but with one distinct and fundamental difference: willingness. While we have been hurt, there is a measure of willingness to love, pray, and forgive our enemies. We just don't know how, and are *unskilled* in the practice. The people may be long gone or they could be an ongoing presence in our lives. If the people at home, work, and in other parts of our lives continue to open up the scabs of our anger and wounds, figuring out how to forgive them is quite the mountain to climb.

The third perspective is from those who say they have no enemies. The "holds" in their ships are empty. Sure, there might be people they dislike, or who are annoying, but they don't fall in the category of enemy. This is good news. If you are living free of resentment and anger and are in peaceful relationships with your family, friends, coworkers, and world—then bravo, that is extraordinary! You are living right, very fortunate, or just plain lucky! There may come a time when it is different, so be grateful. Experience tells me, though, that if people explore their past, they just might find some cargo hiding in their hold. Or if they spend some time reflecting upon political parties or groups and people on the opposing sides of issues they care about, they discover that to love is difficult for even the most undisturbed people. Either we aren't aware there are people for us to forgive, or we are *blind* to it. While they might not call them enemies, there may be people in their lives who are a burr under their saddle. They are known as "EGR" folks or "extra grace required" people. They can be released too.

The last posture shows itself when people forgive people expeditiously (which is Christ-like), but too quickly reconcile with individuals who are repentant but unwilling or incapable of changing. They seem to neglect their own well-being. I am sure you have known people like this. They are the doormats to manipulators, abusers, and exploiters. They keep going back to chaotic and unhealthy people who inflict damage. There are circumstances for which forgiving your enemies should be done without reconciling with the person(s) who repeatedly hurt you. In situations like these, people should forgive but not forget.

An excellent beginning to allowing God to clean out our hearts so that we can love, whether we have an abundance or a sliver of willingness, is to make the decision that we will forgive.

Decide

Luke tells us that Jesus instructed, "Be merciful, just as your Father is merciful" (Luke 6:36). Matthew records his words as even stronger. Immediately, after teaching the disciples the Lord's Prayer, he says, "For if you forgive others their trespasses, your heavenly Father will also forgive you; but if you do not forgive others, neither will your Father forgive your trespasses" (Matthew 6:14-15).

The Scripture over and over again says that to receive grace, we must offer it. This means that Christians have to learn how to become forgiveness practitioners. You must practice letting go—and it can feel like death. Our egos fight tooth and nail against letting go, especially when the wounds are deep. That's another way to think about forgiving your enemies—you are releasing them over to God. When we forgive, we are letting go of the power that we hold onto over our enemies (and thus the power they hold over us).

We can employ a number of strategies to orient our hearts toward forgiveness. The first we already reviewed. When people hurt us or others, we forget that they bear the divine mark of God. We can't see that in them; all we see is the brokenness and character flaws. However, God has forgiven us, so we in turn forgive. This has to be our code. We forgive as Jesus did.

Another way to develop the skills of being a forgiveness practitioner is trying to see the people who it is hard for us to forgive from a different point of view. The people who hurt us are wounded people (and often, so are we). While we don't and shouldn't like the ways they behave, we can center ourselves on the notion that they are spiritually sick. Holding that perspective from a place of love, rather than a place of feeling superior, will soften our hearts toward the people on our list.

Aside from changing perspective, we also can practice "mental gymnastics." At a previous job, I worked with adults who had abused, neglected, or abandoned their kids. The hardest was to work with the men who had sexually abused kids. Knowing some of the crimes and pain they caused was a struggle. I spoke to a work mentor about it. He suggested that prior to meeting with them, I do some mental gymnastics. He told me to practice visualizing each of them as a small child, seeing them at a very early age, and then to reflect on the possibility that a multitude of things went wrong in the little boys' lives that shaped who they were to become. He then said something very convicting. He said, "These men are broken, flawed, and perpetrated evil. It is terrible. But, if you or I were put in their life circumstances and experience, we would have ended up the same way." In other words, "There but for the grace of God go I." While not excusing or justifying flawed personalities and behavior, seeing our enemies as little unmarked children can help us see them in a different light, as a child of God. Even for the most broken and sinful people, it can help.

And if seeing our enemy as sick or doing mental gymnastics is not sufficient to warrant wanting to forgive, then consider one last thought by theologian Lewis Smedes, who said, "To forgive is to set a prisoner free and discover that the prisoner was you."*

Deciding to forgive is just that . . . a decision. A decision that turns our will over. And in truth, if we are going to love God and neighbor with all our heart, mind, soul, and strength, it should be an easy decision. But we know it isn't. To move onward, you'll need to intentionally engage God and your faith community. And in some circumstances, you may need to seek outside professional help.

Will you decide and see that releasing enemies creates peace? If you can answer yes, then pray to God something along the lines of this:

God, I have decided to forgive. Grant me the power to overcome my unwillingness, the pain or the apathy that would block the power of your redeeming love. I give thanks for the way you have forgiven me. Show me how to extend it to others, whether they are sorry or not. Give me clarity, wisdom, strength, and hope. May the forgiveness I extend point others to your love and power. Amen.

Releasing our enemies will create peace in our hearts. Jesus said, "Come to me, all you that are weary and are carrying heavy burdens, and I will give you rest. Take my yoke upon you, and learn from me; for I am gentle and humble in heart, and you will find rest for your souls. For my yoke is easy, and my burden is light" (Matthew 11:28-30).

If done honestly, we have begun tossing the unneeded and unwanted cargo that our enemies have left us with on our life's voyage.

What next? Put pen to paper.

---

* Lewis Smedes, *Forgive and Forget: Healing the Hurts We Don't Deserve*, eBook, first ed. (San Francisco: Harper & Row, 1984), 133.

Pen and Paper

Inventorying the cargo is a good first step to get rid of it. You'll have an opportunity to do this during one of the reflection days this week. It is optimal to find a quiet place where you can be alone for a time undisturbed. Bring a pen and some sheets of paper. Begin in prayer, and invite God to reveal the people who have been traveling as unwelcomed passengers on your ship, the people whom you need to forgive. As names and pictures of people's faces come to you, write them down. Don't analyze any of it now, just write it down. It will serve you well to go back as far as you remember. Groups, institutions, principles, or anything that sets you off should be included. This is a chance to rid yourself of anything in the past or present that has disturbed your life.

Perhaps it was a kid who relentlessly bullied you thirty years ago when you were a kid, a coworker who undermined your work last week, a vitriolic previous partner, a known gossiper, or a dysfunctional family member. Any person, group, or thing that has been hard to forgive is contributing to the weight in your hold and your capacity to be most useful to God and neighbor! The more cargo you begin to analyze, the better the opportunity your ship could become lighter. Whether your list is long or short, don't fret. God will show you a way to release the negative impact they are having on you.

When families have origins that are unhealthy and dysfunctional—full of chaos, abuse, addiction, instability, or trauma—they justifiably carry heavier freight. If your own story or that of someone you know includes any of this, then you know firsthand the heartbreak and wreckage that come with it. Understandably, people who have hurt us, failed to protect us, or didn't love us in the ways we needed will probably show up on the list (as they should).

Other names will make their way onto your list just as a result of living life. In any relationship there is opportunity for conflict and fracture. Circumstances around messy divorces, financial ruin, job losses, tragedy, betrayals, sickness, or untimely deaths can create enemies. Whether you have a plethora or just a few, it is essential to thoroughly inspect the cargo in our holds, come to know it well, and figure out how to unload it.

If you have your list, you are well on the way. Once our list is made, we must bring it out of our hold and onto the upper deck. Viewing it in the light will reveal important discoveries. We don't want to lose the lesson before it is dumped, as it could provide us growth in love.

We have established that praying for, forgiving, and loving enemies is hard. We have examined common attitudes toward forgiveness. We know that carrying enemies gives us heavy cargo. We have created a list of our baggage by inventorying our enemies. Now it is time to take a closer look. For listing who our enemies are is not enough. Acknowledging the ways they impacted us negatively, what they affect in us and why, our part in creating the problem, and why we continue to allow them to weigh us down are essential if we are to dump the cargo. An example of how we do that is listed at the end of the section.

Opening up and delving into each hurt or resentment will help us to see more clearly. After feeling assured that we have inventoried all the names, groups, or institutions, go back to the list. Beside each name, write out what that person has done to impact your life. Describe why you're angry, the wrongs committed, and your perceptions of the events. Get it in black and white.

After completing the ways in which people made us angry, we have to identify what the anger affected and what we are scared of.

Instincts and Fear

We all have God-given instinctual desires. They are good. But by the nature of being human, they often get out of whack. And when we are at odds with others—or vice versa—usually it is a result of our instincts colliding. Getting our baggage down in writing will enable us to see it in a new way. Six areas are affected when we come into conflict with others: self-esteem, pride, finances, ambitions, personal relationships, and sexual relationships.* Take out your list again and write out the ways your instincts have been affected next to each person. Often you will find a person affects more than one.

After completing that column, the next asks us the penetrating question, "What am I really afraid of?" The answers can shed light on "the why" regarding intense feelings toward the people on our list; in fact, they can often shake us to the core. But God is there to help and can infuse us with the courage to see what's hidden in plain sight.

Enemy	The Origin	Impact	What am I really afraid of?
Ex-spouse	Left me for another	Sex, relationships	I am not good enough.
	Wanted unreasonable financial settlement	Finances	I will not survive financially.
	Told others about me	Pride, self-esteem	Others will think I am at fault.
Coworker	Undermines my work and authority	Ambition, pride	She will convince others I am wrong; I will lose my job.
Relative	Abused me as a child	Personal relationships	I'll never heal.
	Has never taken responsibility	Pride, self-esteem	There will never be justice.†

The Logs in Our Eyes

*"Why do you see the splinter in your brother's or
sister's eye but don't notice the log in your own eye?*

---

* Bill W., *Alcoholics Anonymous*, 65.
† Adapted from Bill W., *Alcoholics Anonymous*, 65.

> *How can you say to your brother or sister, 'Brother,*
> *Sister, let me take the splinter out of your eye,' when*
> *you don't see the log in your own eye? You deceive*
> *yourselves! First take the log out of your eye, and then*
> *you will see clearly to take the splinter out of your*
> *brother's or sister's eye."*
>
> —Luke 6:41-42 CEB

Jesus knew the human tendency to look outward before inward. People see others' faults more clearly than their own. Is it possible that we have a log that's blurring our ability to see (and therefore, love)?

Searching our own faults, motivations, and roles is the most demanding part of inspecting our enemy cargo. It will bring about an increased self-awareness, which at times could be uncomfortable. It takes courage. We'd like to skip this section, but its benefit will outweigh the discomfort. It is true that we most likely have a responsibility in the creation of the resentment.* Sure, many situations aren't entirely our fault, but if we pray and open ourselves up, we can usually discover places where we contributed to the problem. Reviewing the list, we ask where we retaliated; where we were fearful, jealous, or greedy; or when we participated in any of the other sins (pride, envy, gluttony, deceit, lust, or sloth). Writing down the ways we failed in these relationships gives us a humility and understanding and readies us for throwing it overboard. Skipping this crucial part will ensure we focus more on the splinter in others' eyes, rather than the log in our own.

Unload Your Cargo

The cargo has been inspected, brought out from the bowels of our ship onto the upper deck. In the light, we have seen it with new eyes. We have to acknowledge our willingness to forgive and the pain that

---

* I always say that there is one issue for which you are not responsible: child abuse. If you have been abused as a child, it is not your fault. Do not take responsibility. You did not create it. If you are an adult who suffered abuse as a child and haven't gotten the help you need to heal, then that is your part in the resentment.

our enemies have caused us. We have looked at the difficult parts of our own character and makeup. Being able to pray for and love our enemies is nearer than even before. But now it is confession time.

Confession has largely been lost in the church. Most churches don't do Communion every week, choosing to do so monthly or quarterly. And if they do Communion regularly, they leave out the confession and assurance of pardon. We don't like to confess; we'd prefer to keep it private. The Roman Catholic Church considers confession a sacrament. It believes that the faithful should come regularly to God to acknowledge the sins they have committed (by omission or commission) toward God and neighbor, so that they would receive pardon for them. The confession is to be done with a priest, and only that priest can offer absolution. Protestants disagree with that premise, but have largely thrown the baby out with the bathwater, missing out on a transformational practice. Churches would do well to consider how they could learn from Alcoholics Anonymous and the way that it invites its members to "confess." Most Christians' confession practice can be summed up as "I'll tell God and I'll be forgiven." And it's true, God forgives. When we keep all of our wrongs to ourselves, when we don't name our unwillingness to forgive, or tuck away our faults in the shadows, they can remain with us. Our egos can stay largely in control. The deepest of our enemies can stay securely hidden in our cargo. And it continues to weigh us down.

Meeting with a trusted person to share our list will unlock the cage of unforgiveness built with walls of anger, resentment, and hate. It is crucial for each of us to find a person who is trusted and who can hold confidences to share our lives and confess our list. It could be a pastor, priest, trusted friend, therapist, or anyone else who we trust can withhold judgment and create an atmosphere of safety. In and through this holy time, God will cleanse us and allow us to release our feelings to the power of the Spirit.

After sharing the list and all of the items on it, we can pray the following prayer found in the *The Book of Common Prayer* or something like it:

Most merciful God,
we confess that we have sinned against thee
in thought, word, and deed,
by what we have done,
and by what we have left undone.
We have not loved thee with our whole heart;
we have not loved our neighbors as ourselves.
We are truly sorry and we humbly repent.
For the sake of thy Son Jesus Christ,
have mercy on us and forgive us;
that we may delight in thy will,
and walk in thy ways,
to the glory of thy Name. Amen.[*]

Taking a comprehensive inventory of our enemy cargo has not been an easy task. Many of us will feel more at ease after sharing our cargo. We should feel lighter. Freer.

God is merciful to everyone, including those we consider enemies: people who have hurt us or hurt our families, child molesters, rapists, politicians of different stripes, people who hate God, people who love God, people who are trying to destroy us or the world. Jesus' teaching says that we must be merciful too.

The answer to "How do we love our enemy?" is not one-size-fits-all. There is no one process or series of actions that will work for every situation. That is because enemies come in a variety of shapes and sizes. Each circumstance will look different in its application. There are some instances that we will be able to reconcile, and others we shouldn't. Forgiveness is more art than science, but an essential key to loving God and neighbor, regardless. If we are to love God and neighbor, we must forgive.

Now that our process is complete, we can more generously pray for the people on our list and discern ways to love. Sometimes loving will be staying away. Other times, it will be trying to live in harmonious

---

* The Episcopal Church, The Book of Common Prayer (ebook), https://www.episcopalchurch.
  org/book-common-prayer, (New York: Church Publishing Incorporated, 1979), 331,
  accessed August 30, 2018.

relationship again. But one thing is for certain, forgiveness is the key to loving and praying for our enemies.

When we repay evil with good, we will be children of God (see Luke 6:35). And not only that, Jesus' love will be made known through us. I told you it wasn't easy.

In Conclusion

Following Jesus is hard. But God's grace inspires, compels, and enables each of us to grow and deepen our capacity to love God, neighbor, enemy, and ourselves. In community, we must be faithful to spiritual practices, be fruitful in the ways and with whom we spend time, and be surrendered to the results.

Love boldly, love courageously, love those inside and outside your circle, and love those who you think don't deserve to be loved. And by so doing, Jesus Christ will be revealed and glorified.

Week 3
DEVOTIONALS

Day 15: The Opposite

Scripture

> *"You have heard that it was said, 'You shall love your*
> *neighbor and hate your enemy.' But I say to you, Love*
> *your enemies and pray for those who persecute you, so*
> *that you may be children of your Father in heaven; for*
> *he makes his sun rise on the evil and on the good, and*
> *sends rain on the righteous and on the unrighteous.*
> *For if you love those who love you, what reward do*
> *you have? Do not even the tax collectors do the same?*
> *And if you greet only your brothers and sisters, what*
> *more are you doing than others? Do not even the*
> *Gentiles do the same?"*
>
> *—Matthew 5:43-47*

Jesus rightly noted that loving people who love us, people in our family, our friend circle, or church or community is natural. It is easy because they usually have our best interests in mind. You don't have to be a Christian to love in that way. Persons from all religious traditions, agnostics, and atheists love those closest to them. It is not an extraordinary act because it doesn't require much. (Unlike loving those who persecute.) It is a pretty straightforward teaching from Jesus, but harder to live out.

Seinfeld was a popular and beloved comedy series in the 1990s. George Costanza was played by actor Jason Alexander and was one of the key characters along with Jerry Seinfeld. He was a neurotic fellow with many issues and often lived with his parents. Usually things didn't go right for George because he made poor decisions. In the eighty-sixth episode titled "The Opposite," he came to the conclusion that every decision he had made had been wrong. His life was the opposite of what it could be. Jerry, the main character, asserted that he should do the exact opposite of what his instincts were. Whatever comes into his mind should be turned upside down. That would make things in his life right! George bought in, and it paid off right away. He ordered the opposite of his normal lunch and then consequently saw a beautiful woman who had ordered the same thing. He introduced himself to her by saying, "My name is George. I'm unemployed and I live with my parents." To his surprise and delight, she was impressed and goes out with him. In the end, it ultimately didn't work out for George, but we can glean an important lesson from this unreformed, fictional character.

Every instinct of ours cries out to not pray for our enemies. Our thoughts revolve around getting justice, vengeance, or apathy. As people called to love God and neighbor, we must "George Costanza" our enemies—suspend our unwillingness and pray. If you have done the work of the chapter, then you have a list. Pull it out now and read over the names you have recorded in the first column. (If you haven't yet done so, you'll find the exercise on pages 102–103.)

Lift up each individual to God, praying that God would come to them in the exact way they need. If you still have resistance, pray simply for God to soften your heart toward them and that "Your will, not mine, be done."

Romans says, "For if while we were enemies, we were reconciled to God through the death of his Son, much more surely, having been reconciled, will we be saved by his life" (Romans 5:10). Paul uses some strong language about the way God reconciled us through Jesus Christ while we were still apart from him. God has loved us extravagantly and he wants us to love in the same extravagant way—even those on our list.

Prayer

Thank you, God, for your call to love those who persecute, and for the way it gives us a picture into your extravagant grace. Amen.

Challenge

**To "do the opposite" toward your enemies.
Pray for the people on your list.**

Day 16: Mourning Comes

Scripture

> *"Blessed are those who mourn, for they will be comforted."*
>
> —*Matthew 5:4*

Many years ago I served at a local nonprofit as the director of a resource center for fathers. One day a man arrived at my office and asked to speak to whoever was in charge. The unscheduled visit turned out to be one of the most memorable visits that I have ever had. I noticed his intensity as soon as he crossed the threshold into my office. It was palpable. I invited him to sit down and asked him what brought him in today. Over the next thirty or so minutes, I would learn why. He was possibly the angriest human being that I ever met and his demeanor was consistent even through e-mail when he contacted me after our initial meeting (writing mostly in ALL CAPS).

He first heard about us because we offered a monthly legal workshop for dads who were struggling with custody and child support issues. He hadn't seen his children in a long time, and his anger was barely contained. Veins were popping out of his neck, and it was as though he was clenching the arms of the chair with all of his might. To say the man was angry would be like saying a volcano has elevated temperatures. He described in detail all the people who wronged him, and no one in his life seemed to be excluded. He cataloged the wrongs from his ex-wife, the courts, his judge, the child support office, police officers, and so on. He went on and on and had very little insight into his own participation in creating the issues, but I didn't think it would be helpful (or safe) to point any of that out. Especially since I learned, if I were to believe his report (and I did), that when he was scheduled to be at the courthouse, he was required to have an escort because of a prior threat he made to a judge.

I inquired if he had sought out assistance from any other agencies that offered help to fathers. That's when he snapped. He was so frustrated that he came up out of his chair aggressively, with his hands on my desk leaning in toward me with gritted teeth, asserting that no one wanted to help him and no one cared about the fact that he hadn't seen his kids. It was a particularly intense moment. I probably should have been scared, but I wasn't. I responded in a way that retrospectively seems very unwise. I said something to the effect of "I can see why no one wants to help you when you act like that. It makes me not want to help you. But, what I really sense is that you are really sad because you love your kids, you are afraid that you won't see them again, and are so frustrated and discouraged you don't know what else to do. I am sorry you are suffering."

The anger and hatred etched in his contorted face and in the fire in his eyes melted away in an instant. What came forth was mourning. His eyes filled with tears and he was able to tap into what he had hidden from the world and probably even himself: pain.

Frederick Buechner said, "Whenever you find tears in your eyes, especially unexpected tears, it is well to pay the closest attention."[*]

I am not sure he did pay such close attention. He kept in touch with me for a few years after this encounter. During those contacts, his circumstances didn't change. I suspect that he still resides inside the prison that his hatred constructed.

But his story has a message for us. Even though we may not identify with his circumstances, the intensity of his anger and frustration, or

---

[*] The Frederick Buechner Center, "Listening to Your Life," http://www.frederickbuechner.com /listening-to-your-life/, accessed August 31, 2018.

have the long list of nemeses who have negatively impacted our lives, we too have feelings underneath any disdain, resentment, moral superiority, or hatred of our enemies. It does not matter whether it is prominent or restrained, we too have pain; and we'd best pay close attention.

Blessed are those who mourn.

Wherever you are in the journey of loving and forgiving your enemies, whether or not you have a willingness to forgive, acknowledging both the presence of our anger toward the people who have hurt us and the pain that has resulted can be a first step. It doesn't feel blessed to mourn, but we must be in contact with our sadness and grief for them to be transformed. We can call on God, our faith community, or outside support as we acknowledge and engage these feelings. As we begin to embark on this narrow road, God will meet us where we are, but won't leave us there.... For *you* will be comforted.

Acknowledging the reality of pain begins the process of reconciliation to God, to ourselves, and to others.

Prayer

God, I offer the people who are weighing me down to you. If the pain I have is holding me from deeper love, please show me the way to acknowledge it, transform it, and ultimately be a testament to your goodness and love. Amen.

Challenge
To pray and offer God any pain or fear
that is undergirding anger toward others.
And to pray again for the people on your list.

Day 17: What's That in Your Eye?

Scripture

> *"Don't judge, so that you won't be judged. You'll*
> *receive the same judgment you give. Whatever you*

> *deal out will be dealt out to you. Why do you see*
> *the splinter that's in your brother's or sister's eye, but*
> *don't notice the log in your own eye? How can you*
> *say to your brother or sister, 'Let me take the splinter*
> *out of your eye,' when there's a log in your eye? You*
> *deceive yourself! First take the log out of your eye, and*
> *then you'll see clearly to take the splinter out of your*
> *brother's or sister's eye."*
>
> *—Matthew 7:1-5 CEB*

I had 20/20 vision up until the retina in my right eye became partially torn. It was a serious injury that the doctor warned could lead to blindness if not properly cared for. The treatment and recovery were long. My eye was dilated for six months. Miraculously, not only did my vision return to normal, but it improved. It was better than 20/20 in the injured eye. My doctor was amazed. I felt a smidgen prideful about it. I liked to say that I could see very clearly. Well, that lasted about five years. I ignored the signs: blurriness when looking at digital clocks and pervasive squinting when I would watch television. My wife began to point out my squinting and suggested that I get my eyes checked out. I was resistant, saying, "I have very good vision, better than 20/20." I wanted to hold on to the belief that I still could see better than others. I couldn't. Finally, I relented and discovered what everyone else knew, I needed glasses for astigmatism in both eyes.

As soon as I put those glasses on, my life was so much better. Everything was sharper and crisper. I could see clearly. That's what Jesus was talking about with the log in our own eye. Jesus wants us to see ourselves and others—including our enemies—without blurriness. While it is more satisfying and much easier to see the faults and character flaws in others, we must first look at ourselves. When people wrong us, we get angry at them, and we make all kinds of judgments about their behavior. We assign their mistakes to their lack of character and totally dismiss or minimize any role that we might have had. But when we inevitably fall short or fail, we resist assuming the blame and have a tendency to assign the mistake to our circumstances rather than our character (which is the opposite that we do for others).

The truth is uncovered as we examine our relationships with the enemies we have, and it is this: very often we have had a part of creating the problem or situation. In many cases we can't assume all of the blame, but if we explore it more closely, we can find where different choices or a different reaction could have contributed to a different result. In other words, we must look inward before projecting blame outward.

Prayer

God, I offer to you the ways I have fallen short. Whether I have sinned boldly or not, forgive me for my trespasses and shortcomings. Show me the way forward and shape me in the ways that would point others to the power of your transformational love. Amen.

Challenge

To confess to God the faults that contribute to your troubles. And to pray again for the people on your list.

Day 18: Our Own Worst Enemy

Scripture

> *"Blessed are the merciful, for they will receive mercy."*
> —*Matthew 5:7*

Throughout this week we have been looking at ways we can pray, forgive, and love our enemies. The purpose of all this laborious work is to open up the channels of grace and mercy within us so that we can more fully live the Greatest Commandment. And it is challenging work for most of us. Yet, some people struggle with an enemy so near, it is hidden in plain sight: the person who stares back in the mirror.

I met a woman one time after she came to a worship service. She said that it was important that she meet with me after hearing something about forgiveness in the message. During the meeting, she revealed that she had intense guilt and regret that was weighing her down. Through her tears, she shared that she had had an abortion as a teen and was haunted by the decision. Forgiveness for herself and from God seemed impossible. She thought that God might decide to punish her for her decision made many years ago. She was not able to connect that God's forgiveness was readily available. What she could not also see is that to believe that God couldn't forgive is a hidden form of pride. Believing those lies keeps us separate from love. This poor woman was being punished not for her sins, but by them.

She is not the first or last person to believe the lie. The old saying, "We have met the enemy, and he is us" applies to people who struggle to be merciful to themselves. Their circumstances and experiences may take a different shape, but patterns are often the same. A deep sense of guilt arises since we know that we have failed or hurt others. That is normal and God-given. Over time, the inner critic begins to wage war, offering up much evidence from the past that reinforces our failure. It replays on repeat and we come to the belief that we are too broken, damaged, or sinful to be forgiven by God. Shame sets in and we believe the lie that the forgiveness found in Jesus doesn't apply, perhaps because the pain we feel is so great.

God's grace found in Jesus Christ is bigger than anything that they have done or failed to do. If that is you, can you find a way to love the enemy within?

Prayer

Merciful God, come to my assistance. Show me the way to mercy so I may experience the depth and power of your love that proclaims that I am forgiven. And by so doing, may I forgive myself and others. In Christ's name I pray. Amen.

Challenge

To forgive yourself and remember that no failing needs to separate you from forgiveness. And to pray again for the people on your list.

Day 19: Relinquishing Power

Scripture

Do not fret because of those who are evil
  or be envious of those who do wrong;
for like the grass they will soon wither,
  like green plants they will soon die away.

Trust in the LORD *and do good;*
  dwell in the land and enjoy safe pasture.
Take delight in the LORD,
  and he will give you the desires of your heart.

Commit your way to the LORD;
  trust in him and he will do this:
He will make your righteous reward shine like the dawn,
  your vindication like the noonday sun.

Be still before the LORD
  and wait patiently for him;
do not fret when people succeed in their ways,
  when they carry out their wicked schemes.

Refrain from anger and turn from wrath;
  do not fret—it leads only to evil.
For those who are evil will be destroyed,
  but those who hope in the LORD *will inherit the land.*
  —Psalm 37:1-9 NIV

God knows we get angry and often for good reason. If we are rooted in anger and not in our trust of God, the psalmist astutely acknowledges that it will lead to evil. Perhaps you don't think so. Holy anger, when rightly directed, is a good thing. There are examples of this throughout history and maybe even in our lives. But it is also true that righteous anger has been foolishly applied. We have said the wrong thing at the most inopportune time or have done something from a place of spite. Evidence in history also points to righteous anger being misapplied.

117

The name "Lucifer," if we remember, means "bearer of light." That means that evil always disguises itself as justice, good, or getting what one deserves. If that is so, then perhaps some of the ways that we and our culture apply holy anger disguise themselves as good, but actually aren't.

Can I give up the holy anger I have toward anyone on my list (or even myself)?

I'd rather hold on to what the psalmist says about evildoers; that "they will soon wither, like green plants they will soon die away" (Psalm 37:2 NIV). When I get in hopeful anticipation of my enemies to wither, I must remind myself of Proverbs 24:17, which says, "Do not rejoice when your enemies fall, and do not let your heart be glad when they stumble."

Our minds and hearts experience something akin to a magnetic pull toward anger. It comes in the form of outrage, apathy, or confrontation. Giving up the anger we have toward our enemies and our hopeful anticipation of their demise feels like death. Throw these feelings overboard anyway. Step out into a new unknown where the power that they have can no longer wound, because of Jesus Christ. As you continue to make that decision, even as your willingness ebbs and flows, you will notice the still small whisper of the Divine inviting you toward trusting deeper and doing good.

Live that life that is worthy of your calling.

Prayer

Holy One, I offer my anger, holy or otherwise, to You. Take all of it, what I know and I what I don't, along with any apprehension I have to hold on to it. Transform it and make it into what you want. Deepen my reliance upon you and make me trust. Direct my actions toward good, showing me ways to love you, the ones I oppose, and myself. Amen.

Challenge

To give the power you hold over your enemies to the One who has power, God. And to pray again for the people on your list.

Day 20: Living Forgiveness

Scripture

> "I am the vine, you are the branches. Those who abide
> in me and I in them bear much fruit, because apart
> from me you can do nothing."
>
> —*John 15:5*

You can do it. That's the message I pray you take away from these twenty-one days together. You engaged in spiritual practices; you stretched in new areas. You walked through a challenging process that helps unload unwanted, heavy baggage, all to more fully follow Jesus Christ.

You can do it... because of Christ. The message from the Scripture reminds us of our Source. Jesus Christ is the vine, and we are the branches. From the Source comes fruit. That means that our ability to love God, neighbor, and enemy comes not from us but from the divine. God in us nurtures the willingness to act and infuses us with the power to live forgiveness for the long haul. And we will need it, because many future opportunities will present themselves.

To remain connected:

1. Keep up the spiritual disciplines. We stay connected to Christ by engaging in spiritual practices of prayer and meditation, Scripture reading and reflection, financial generosity, small group community, communal worship, and serving others. These practices keep us aligned.
2. Remember your need before God.
3. Pray on your knees regularly—it communicates humility.
4. Picture your enemies as children and remember that they are spiritually sick.
5. Stay vigilant to guard against resentment, anger, and moral superiority. Release the need to be right.
6. When people hurt you, forgive anyway.

And in all things, *trust God*.

Prayer

God, thank you for giving us Jesus as the perfect example of loving God, neighbor, and enemy. I trust you to be with us as we try to emulate him and to forgive us when we fail. Amen.

Challenge

**To make a plan to put the practices
you've learned into your everyday life,
and to pray once again for your enemies.**

Day 21: Rest and Trust

Scripture 1:

> *And on the seventh day God finished the work that he had done, and he rested on the seventh day from all the work that he had done. So God blessed the seventh day and hallowed it, because on it God rested from all the work that he had done in creation.*
>
> —Genesis 2:2-3

Scripture 2:

> *Remember the sabbath day, and keep it holy.*
> —Exodus 20:8

God finished the work he had done and rested on the seventh day. Apparently, the rest of us have a hard time remembering and keeping the sabbath because we trick ourselves into believing that our work is never done. My fairly intense, type-A personality has served me well in a variety of ways, but not without a price. One of my favorite sayings is "Fail forward *faster*. Figure out what doesn't work and stop doing it." I often move decisively, getting things done, and crossing things off the to-do list. Two problems: first, the to-do list is never completed. Second, rest never was on my to-do list.

This truth stings…too much of a good thing ends up not being a good thing. I suspect that remembering the sabbath and keeping it holy for many modern folks is right up there with loving your enemies. We say we crave a slower pace, but in reality our talons are deeply buried into our love and need for busyness, movement, and full schedules— especially on the weekends.

The sabbath is designed to create rest, connection with God and your loved ones, and to worship. By doing so, you will replenish your reserves so you can do the most important work of your life, to love God and neighbor.

Prayer

On this day God, I offer myself to you. Take away any need I have to be busy. May I be present to the people I love, disengage from work, and remember that you are the God of love, whose burden is light. Amen.

Challenge

To rest and connect with the value of recharging.

LEADER HELPS

LEADER HELPS

Welcome to *The Jesus Challenge* group study experience! This three-week study is designed so that it could be taken on independently, though the accountability and Christian community of a group leads to more engagement and a richer understanding. While the challenge itself is designed to encapsulate three weeks, I recommend meeting for an introductory session, during which the group can discuss the challenge on which they are soon to embark and take time to absorb the rich information found in the book's introduction.

By leading this group study, you are guiding people through an experience that will help people to be faithful, fruitful, and surrendered. The challenge is designed to have people engage in spiritual practices, be attentive to the ways they invest time, and leave the results up to God.

As group leader, your role will be to facilitate the group sessions, creating a safe environment for all group members to grow. All groups are different in composition, and the next few pages will offer guidance for any of them, no matter how different. *Note: Ideal group size is eight to twelve participants.*

The study with a suggested introductory session makes use of the following components:

- the book *The Jesus Challenge: 21 Days to Loving God and Neighbor*, by Justin LaRosa, and
- the video segments on the companion DVD.

In addition to the study book, group members will need Bibles (print or electronic). The suggested introductory session will enable all participants to be introduced to the study and prepare for the next meeting by reading the Introduction material. (Often participants don't read prior to the first group gathering.)

Each chapter will have an opening section followed by seven daily reflections, which include Scripture, practical application, a prayer, and a challenge.

Below is an outline of two format options for structuring your group time. You may wish to follow one of the proposed formats, or you may choose to adapt them to meet your unique needs. The times listed are estimates and can be altered according to the flow and pace of your group.

60-Minute Option

Welcome/Sign In/Goals . . . . .2 minutes
Opening Prayer . . . . 1 minute
Biblical Foundation . . . . .2 minutes
Video . . . . .10 minutes
Discussion. . . . . .35 minutes
Looking Ahead to Next Week . . . . .5 minutes
Take-Home Message/Closing Prayer. . . . . .5 minutes

90-Minute Option

Welcome/Sign In/Goals . . . . .2 minutes
Opening Prayer . . . . 1 minute
Biblical Foundation . . . . .2 minutes
Video . . . . .20 minutes
Contemplative Practice
(Centering Prayer/*Lectio Divina*). . . . . .20 minutes
Discussion. . . . . .35 minutes
Looking Ahead to Next Week . . . . .5 minutes
Take-Home Message/Closing Prayer. . . . . .5 minutes

General Instructions for Facilitating a Group

Preparation and Timing

The more prepared you are as the leader, the better the experience will be for the group. There will be things to do in advance of the session. Read all the chapters and complete the daily devotions. Select and highlight parts that impacted you. Be sure to prepare any materials for the class ahead of time, including a way to view the videos.

Be prepared to keep track of time so that you can fit in all elements of the meeting.

Confidentiality

To create a safe environment, confidentiality will need to be agreed upon and kept. The facilitator should set the tone and remind the group in all sessions, "What is said here stays here." The facilitator may also want to review the limits of confidentiality.

Welcome/Sign In

Depending on the level of formality or familiarity among members in the group, you may choose to have group members sign in and pick up a name tag. You can ask for their names, e-mail addresses, and phone numbers in order to create a group roster so that in the following weeks they may simply check their names on the roster to sign in. Even if you have participants sign up online or pre-register for the group in some other way, signing in each week will help you to keep track of attendance so that you may follow up with those who have missed.

Session Goals

Provide a verbal outline of the goals for each weekly session (you also might choose to write these on a board or chart). These are included in your leader helps.

Introductions

In the suggested introductory session or during Week 1, the facilitator can ask participants to share their names, two facts about themselves (this can be anything they want to share about themselves, including how they found their way to this group), and one hope they have for the small group experience. The facilitator should set the example by going first, giving a brief response.

Note: If you have fewer than ten people, do the introductions together. If your group is larger than ten people, you may want to break into small groups for sharing in order to keep things moving.

Opening Prayer

The opening prayer can be done in a variety of different ways. You can bring a printed prayer for the group to read in unison, offer a spontaneous prayer, or have a group member offer a prayer. (After the first session, you may choose to recruit group members to offer the opening and closing prayers. This is an excellent way to get everyone involved.)

Biblical Foundation

This is the foundational Scripture passage for the session. Invite a group member to read it aloud each week. You might consider having one person read it from one translation and another read from a different translation. Additionally, it can be used for the optional contemplative exercise.

Video

Each week has a video segment that sets up the week. Be prepared to have the correct equipment.

Optional Activity—*Lectio Divina,* Centering Prayer

If you follow the 90-minute format, this section outlines an additional activity for the group. It suggests two different contemplative methods: group *Lectio Divina* and group centering prayer.

Video, Chapter, and Devotion Discussion

Whether you follow the 60-minute or 90-minute plan, engaging group members in reviewing and discussing the readings and devotions is critical to the effectiveness of the group session. Alerting participants that you will be reviewing the readings and devotions in each session increases the likelihood that they will complete them.

The Video, Chapter, and Devotion Discussion is designed to help the group dig deeper into the topic for the week. There are question for you to use to stimulate discussion. For example, you might ask the group after the video, "What struck you in the video?" There are discussion questions for each chapter that you can use to facilitate discussion, or you might highlight during your preparation and reading aspects of the chapter or devotion to discuss. If the group is larger than ten people, you may want to break into small groups for the discussion and activity.

Looking Ahead to Next Week

Each session allows time for discussing the upcoming week's topic. Talk briefly about the topic, identify the pages in the book participants need to read and complete before the next session, including the devotions. Cover any special preparation required for the coming week.

Take-Home Message/Closing Prayer

At the conclusion of the session, have each participant share his or her "Take-Home Message"—the key message that he or she will take home from the group session. Don't be afraid of silence. If no one shares after ten seconds, ask, "Would anyone be willing to share first?" If no one responds after an additional five to ten seconds, provide an answer. Then ask for other comments. You might choose to facilitate the Take-Home Message while the group is standing in a circle holding hands prior to the closing prayer.

Suggested Introductory Session

An introductory session will not follow the same format of the other sessions, as there will be more time for introductions and reading the book's introduction (assuming the books are distributed at this meeting and participants haven't read them ahead of time).

If your group is not having an introductory session, you will want to incorporate introductory elements into your first session.

60 Minutes

Welcome/Sign In/Goals . . . . 2 minutes
Participant Introductions . . . . 20 minutes
Opening Prayer . . . . 1 minute
Biblical Foundation . . . . 2 minutes
Book Introduction . . . . 15 minutes
Discussion . . . . 10 minutes
Looking Ahead to Next Week . . . . 5 minutes
Take-Home Message/Closing Prayer . . . . 5 minutes

Welcome/Sign In

- Invite participants to sign in and make a name tag. If the group is smaller and seated around a table, tent cards are another option for names.
- Briefly introduce yourself and provide a warm welcome to the group.
- Provide the dates and times for the group sessions and review any other housekeeping items.
- Distribute copies of the book. Explain that there are seven days of readings and devotions for each week as well as Methodical Prayer, which may be completed in thirty to forty-five minutes each day. Encourage group members to complete their reading prior to each weekly session.

Review the Session Goals

1. Get to know the participants and the resources, and discuss the expectations of the group experience.

2. Understand and identify the season of life for each participant and any obstacles that are getting in the way of our love for God.

3. Commit to Methodical Prayer, making the gratitude list, reading the chapters, and completing the daily devotions.

Participant Introductions

Share names, two facts about yourself, and one hope for the group experience.

Opening Prayer

Offer an opening prayer.

Biblical Foundation

Matthew 22:36-40

Read and Review Book Introduction

- Talk about how following Jesus is a challenge.
- Review the three obstacles to love, highlighting how each obstacle—forgetfulness, distraction, and self-sufficiency— impedes the call to love God and neighbor.
- Review the antidotes to the obstacles, highlighting how being faithful to spiritual practices; being fruitful in the ways and with whom we invest our time; and being surrendered to the results of our efforts can open us up to deeper love.

Discussion

- How have forgetfulness, distraction, and self-sufficiency affected your relationship with God and the call to love God and neighbor?
- What spiritual practices are you familiar with or are already engaging in?
- Discuss Methodical Prayer, found on pages 19–21. Do you think this will be difficult? Why? What can you do to ensure the most meaningful prayer time?

Looking Ahead to Next Week

Talk briefly about chapter 1. Identify the pages to read and where the daily devotions are located.

Take-Home Message/Closing Prayer

- Have each participant share his or her "Take-Home Message."
- Offer a closing prayer.

Week 1

If you did not hold an introductory session, incorporate more extensive introductions and add in time for discussing the book's introduction.

Welcome/Sign In/Introductions (If Needed)

Review the Session Goals

1. Discuss ways to know and experience God through the spiritual practices of worship, Scripture reflection, and prayer.
2. Review Methodical Prayer, the seasons of life, and the spiritual fuel tank metaphor.
3. Identify the current season of your life and the level in your spiritual tank.

Opening Prayer

Offer an opening prayer.

Biblical Foundation

- Luke 10:25-28
- Matthew 22:34-40
- Mark 12:28-34

Video

Show the video associated with the week.

Video, Chapter, and Devotion Discussion

1. What struck you in the video?
2. What are your obstacles to living the Greatest Commandment?
3. In which season—plenty, difficulty, or ordinary—is it easiest to express your love for God? In which is it most difficult? In which season do you feel closest to God? Reflect upon different seasons you've experienced and share, if comfortable doing so, how your relationship with God was affected.
4. After reflecting upon the different seasons, which would you say that you are currently in?
5. How can you love God in times of plenty, during difficulties, and in the ordinary?
6. What is the current level in your tank? How often are you visiting the filling station? Is it easier for you to connect to God in difficulty, or is it the time when you shy away? What does going to God in difficult times to fill your tank look like? Which spiritual disciplines connect you to God the most?
7. Was there a devotion that impacted you this week?

Looking Ahead to Next Week

Talk briefly about chapter 2. Identify the pages to read and where the daily devotions are located.

Take-Home Message/Closing Prayer

- Have each participant share his or her "Take-Home Message."
- Offer a closing prayer.

Week 2

Welcome/Sign In

Review the Session Goals

1. Discuss and review the meaning of the good Samaritan.

2. Identify the places where you feel compassion for those outside your circle.
3. Review the process for identifying and loving your neighbor:
   - see those who suffer,
   - experience compassion for those outside our circle,
   - draw near to those in need, and
   - act.

Opening Prayer

Offer an opening prayer.

Biblical Foundation

- Luke 10:29-37
- Deuteronomy 6:5
- Leviticus 19:18

Video

- Show the video associated with the week.
- *Optional*: Watch an online clip of the Mister Rogers episode mentioned in the chapter.

Video, Chapter, and Devotion Discussion

1. What struck you in the video?
2. When you hear the word *Samaritan*, what are the words that first come to your mind? After learning about how scandalous Jesus' use of a Samaritan in the story was to the lawyer, who are other modern-day "Samaritans"?
3. Who are the people whom you would rather pass on the other side of the road? Who is suffering in your community that everyone seems to be ignoring?

4. Where do you look at the world and your heart breaks? Where do you look at your local community and feel anger? Where does your heart feel compassion for those on the margins?
5. What are your spiritual gifts?
6. Where might you go to journey outside your current circles?
7. Was there a devotion that impacted you this week?

Looking Ahead to Next Week

Talk briefly about chapter 3. Identify the pages to read and where the daily devotions are located.

Take-Home Message/Closing Prayer

- Have each participant share his or her "Take-Home Message."
- Offer a closing prayer.

Week 3

Welcome/Sign In

Review the Session Goals

1. Review why the call to forgive enemies is crucial to loving God and neighbor.
2. Review and discuss the postures we take toward forgiveness.
3. Review the process of forgiveness and explore next steps.

Opening Prayer

Offer an opening prayer.

Biblical Foundation

- Luke 6:27-36

Video

Show the video associated with the week.

Video, Chapter, and Devotion Discussion

1. What struck you in the video?
2. Who are the people stored as unwelcome cargo in your hold?
3. Who are your enemies? Are there people whom you need to forgive?
4. What posture of forgiveness do you generally take?
5. Describe a time when you forgave and felt free.
6. What could be a next step for you?
7. Was there a devotion that impacted you this week?

Take-Home Message/Closing Prayer

- Have each participant share his or her "Take-Home Message" from the entire experience.
- Offer a final closing prayer.

APPENDICES

Appendix A
CENTERING PRAYER*

About Centering Prayer

The purpose of centering prayer is not to create peace or empty your mind, but to cultivate relationship with God through silence. The focus of centering prayer is the desire to be with God, who is within you, to allow God to work within you, and to silently surrender to God's love.

Basil Pennington's Method of Centering Prayer†

1. Sit relaxed and be quiet.
2. Be in faith and love to God who dwells in the center of your being.
3. Take up a love word and let it be gently present, supporting your being to God in faith-filled love.
4. Whenever you become aware of anything, simply, gently return to the Lord with the use of your prayer word.

---

* Taken from James A. Harnish and Justin LaRosa, *A Disciple's Heart (Daily Workbook)* (Nashville: Abingdon Press, 2015), 120.

† Adapted from M. Basil Pennington, *Centering Prayer: Renewing an Ancient Christian Prayer Form* (New York: Doubleday, 2001), xv, xvi.

Another way to describe this method:

1. Be with God within.
2. Use a word to stay.
3. Use the word to return.

Instructions for a Time of Centering Prayer

1. Select your centering word. It can be any word to focus on as you pray (e.g., *light, love, Jesus, mercy, peace*). You will keep this word throughout the prayer period. When/if your mind wanders, return gently to your centering word.
2. Ensure you are in a location that is quiet and as distraction-free as possible. Sit with your back straight in a chair, feet on the floor, and your hands positioned comfortably on your legs.
3. Read a short passage of Scripture—perhaps one of the readings from the week's devotionals. Then shut your eyes and begin the prayer period. Generally, centering prayer is done for twenty minutes, but you could start with ten or fifteen and work your way up.
4. Say your centering word silently for the allotted time.
5. Conclude by praying the Lord's Prayer aloud.

Appendix B
*LECTIO DIVINA**

About *Lectio Divina*

Lectio Divina (pronounced lektīō dĭvīnə), which means "Divine Reading," is an ancient practice of contemplative Bible study that allows the Bible to read you rather than you reading the Bible. There are generally four movements or steps in *Lectio Divina*:

1. *Lectio*: A slow, meditative reading of Scripture.
2. *Meditatio*: Thinking or reflecting on the word or phrase. (Why did it stand out? Why did it strike your heart?)
3. *Oratio*: Responding to the word or phrase. Tell God how you feel and what you think.
4. *Contemplatio*: Resting in God in silence—without words, thoughts, or images.

Instructions for a Time of *Lectio Divina*

Say a silent prayer, believing that God is going to speak to you.

---

* Taken from James A. Harnish and Justin LaRosa, *A Disciple's Heart (Daily Workbook)* (Nashville: Abingdon Press, 2015), 119.

1. (*Lectio*) Select a short passage of Scripture, ideally no more than five verses, and read it aloud slowly three times (or listen as a group leader reads it aloud to you). Scripture is meant to be heard with the ears and the soul.
2. During the first reading, listen for context.
3. As you are listening intently during the second and third readings, wait until a word or phrase from the Scripture touches your heart. At that point, stop. You have received the word or phrase from God. Write it down.
4. (*Meditatio*) Say the word or phrase to yourself and begin to reflect on it.
5. Think about why that word or phrase struck you. Ask yourself, *Why did it strike my heart? How is it pertinent to my life?*
6. Record how the word or phrase is speaking to you.
7. (*Oratio*) Respond to the word or phrase from your heart
8. Tell God your feelings either by writing (below or in a journal) or talking silently to God.
9. (*Contemplatio*) Rest in God in silence.[*]
10. As your mind begins to wander, use the word or phrase God gave you to center yourself again.

[*] Taken from James A. Harnish and Justin LaRosa, *A Disciple's Heart (Daily Workbook)* (Nashville: Abingdon Press, 2015), 65.